WHY LABOR ORGANIZING SHOULD BE A CIVIL RIGHT

WHY LABOR ORGANIZING SHOULD BE A CIVIL RIGHT

Rebuilding a Middle-Class Democracy
by Enhancing Worker Voice

Richard D. Kahlenberg and Moshe Z. Marvit

With a Preface by Thomas Geoghegan

The Century Foundation Press • New York

LIBRARY OF CONGRESS CATALOGING-IN-PUBLICATION DATA

Kahlenberg, Richard D.

Why labor organizing should be a civil right : rebuilding a middle-class democracy by enhancing worker voice / Richard D. Kahlenberg and Moshe Z. Marvit ; with a preface by Thomas Geoghegan.

p.   cm.

ISBN 978-0-87078-523-8 (alk. paper)

1. Labor laws and legislation—United States. 2. Employee rights—United States. 3. United States. National Labor Relations Act. 4. Labor unions—Law and legislation—United States. 5. Labor movement—United States. I. Marvit, Moshe Zvi. II. Title.

KF3455.K33 2012
331.25'96—dc23

2011053162

Manufactured in the United States of America

Cover design by Lili Schwartz; cover photo © Richard L. Copley
Text design by Electronic Quill Publishing Services

Foreword

When Occupy Wall Street began helping to shine a powerful spotlight on the nation's growing economic inequality, some criticized the movement for not providing enough concrete policy proposals. But I argued that we should congratulate people in the parks for raising greater awareness of the enormous income and wealth gaps in the United States, and that it is the obligation of progressive think tanks, such as The Century Foundation, to offer workable, forward-looking solutions. This book helps provide one important answer to the pressing question: What, concretely, can be done about the burgeoning economic divide in the United States and the shrinking of the American middle-class?

Of the many causes of increased inequality—globalization, changes in technology, and the adoption of regressive tax policies—the virtual collapse of the American labor movement ranks as a significant, if under-analyzed, problem. As *Why Labor Organizing Should Be a Civil Right* demonstrates, the de-unionization of America is not an inevitable result of larger economic trends; other leading nations maintain both vibrant unions and strong economic growth.

The Century Foundation has long recognized the important role of organized labor in developing broadly shared prosperity, and our concerns go to the very roots of our organization. In 1934, in the midst of the Great Depression, our founder, Edward A. Filene, set up a committee on labor and charged it with preparing a report containing legislative recommendations for strengthening the collective bargaining rights of American workers. The committee then worked closely with the office of

Senator Robert F. Wagner in drafting what would become the National Labor Relations Act.

In more recent years, Century assembled a group of distinguished leaders as part of its Task Force on the Future of Unions, which issued a report, *What's Next for Organized Labor?* (Century Foundation Press, 1999). As part of its ongoing efforts, Century also supported James K. Galbraith's *Created Unequal: The Crisis in American Pay* (Free Press, 1998); Paul Osterman's *Securing Prosperity: The American Labor Market: How It Has Changed and What to Do about It* (Princeton University Press, 1999); Theda Skocpol's *The Missing Middle: Working Families and the Future of American Social Policy* (W. W. Norton, 2000); Jonas Pontusson's *Inequality and Prosperity: Social Europe vs. Liberal America* (Cornell University Press, 2005); and Amy Dean and David B. Reynolds' book, *A New New Deal: How Regional Activism Will Reshape the American Labor Movement* (Cornell University Press, 2010).

This book, *Why Labor Organizing Should Be a Civil Right,* analyzes the antiquated laws that fail to protect individuals who try to exercise their right to organize a union, and recommends that labor organizing be protected under a much more effective statute, the Civil Rights Act of 1991. The book's authors are Richard D. Kahlenberg, a senior fellow at Century, and Moshe Z. Marvit, a labor and civil rights attorney. Kahlenberg is the author most recently of a biography of teacher union leader (and former Century Foundation Trustee) Albert Shanker, who emphasized the important connections between organized labor and public education as twin engines of social mobility in America. Thomas Geoghegan, a well-known labor lawyer and author, who has long championed the idea of making labor organizing a civil right, graciously provides a preface to the book.

On behalf of the Trustees of The Century Foundation, I thank Richard Kahlenberg, Moshe Marvit, and Thomas Geoghegan for this important contribution to the larger effort to strengthen our middle-class American democracy.

—Janice Nittoli, *President*
The Century Foundation
February 2012

Contents

Preface

What should follow Occupy Wall Street? Here is the best possible cause: protecting the right to join a labor union, freely and fairly, without being fired. Nothing would do more to put a brake on the country's runaway inequality. But what kind of labor law reform might inspire such a movement?

Set out in this volume is a well-researched, well-argued case for amending the Civil Rights Act of 1991 to ban discharge, discipline, and other employment discrimination against Americans for giving support to formation of a union. Some would argue that the civil rights movement is an ineffective avenue to pursue such an effort, that the plutocracy that now exists is proof that prior legislation protecting our civil rights against discrimination has failed to achieve the movement's main goal of ensuring real equality. But the authors have in mind a civil right that will do just that—a right that will deliver the ability to bargain over wages, hours and working conditions, a right that would usher in a new legal paradigm that would go way beyond the National Labor Relations Act (NLRA).

The proposal set forth here by Richard Kahlenberg and Moshe Marvit would let workers file suit in federal district courts with their own lawyers to challenge firings and demotions that employers use routinely to shatter union organizing drives. To make this possible, the authors argue for amending—or adding to—the Civil Rights Act of 1991 to outlaw the discrimination that is so crucial in the union-busting or "union-blocking" that has helped reduce the "unionized" share of private sector employment from 35 percent in 1958 to just 6.9 percent today. As it turns out, the authors argue, it is not that we have fallen short of real equality because civil rights laws have failed; rather, it is that the next step has not been taken, because labor laws have been denied the legal remedies— damages, injunctions, discovery, legal fee awards—that make civil rights laws far more effective. The authors aim to fix that.

To be sure, the expansion of labor issues into the civil rights arena raises some questions, but the authors point out that this expansion is not so great a stretch. Today, civil rights laws frequently cover employer-employee relations. With this in mind, it is illogical if this set of laws does not address perhaps the most important part of employer-employee relations: whether employees have a right to be free of discharge or demotion if they want to join a union. In this brief preface, I will address three questions about the relationship of civil rights law to labor law.

Why Not Pursue the Employee Free Choice Act (EFCA), Organized Labor's Own Preferred Remedy?

I am a labor lawyer. I want reform. I am all in favor of the Employee Free Choice Act (EFCA). But it has its limitations—including the problem of being complex and hard to explain to the general public. EFCA calls for card checks without actual union-representation elections and compulsory arbitration by the government of "first contracts." Already, the AFL-CIO has abandoned the idea of card checks without elections ("it's un-American"). And it is dubious that Congress would ever pass a law to let the National Labor Relations Board (NLRB) impose labor contracts on employers ("it's un-American"). One need only consider last summer's uproar in Washington, D.C., over the NLRB's decision to issue an unfair labor practice charge against Boeing for the location of its "Dreamliner" plant in South Carolina. It is hard to imagine arbitrators appointed by a Republican or perhaps even a Democratic president doing any favors for the labor movement; in fact, it is hard to imagine Republican presidents appointing them at all. Even if by some miracle EFCA passes, it would continue to funnel what ought to be a national movement for worker justice at thousands of locations through a single federal agency in Washington, D.C. Throughout Obama's tenure as president, the Senate effectively has tried to shut down the NLRB through filibusters of nominations. Even if EFCA could pass, it would be all the more likely that the NLRB would be held hostage in countless constitutional showdowns.

The great thing about civil rights laws is that Congress turned over their enforcement to working people themselves. There are no novel constitutional problems: it is a legal remedy ready to go. Furthermore, treating labor organizing as a civil right would break the bottleneck of pushing every firing through a single federal agency in Washington, D.C. (even if there are field officers for intake and initial resolutions and hearings). Lose a promotion because you backed a union? If an amended Civil Rights Act protected your right to organize, you could find a lawyer, sign a contingent fee agreement in an hour or two, and file in federal court for a preliminary injunction in just a few days. Will you "win"? Unless dismissed at a threshold stage, most civil rights cases involving employment never go to trial: employers settle. But that is only after discovery—after the workers have an opportunity to subpoena their employers and make them sit through depositions. Under the civil rights laws, the workers would have a power that they have never had under the NLRA—beyond even the dreams of the New Dealers—that is, the power to take testimony and subpoena documents under the very broad discovery rules under modern civil procedure. It is an extraordinary thing about the United States—that individual citizens have such power, if only they can proceed on their own in federal court. In certain respects, an ordinary working American in a federal court has all the investigative power of a federal agency—sometimes more—and no member of Congress, no editorial writer at the *Wall Street Journal,* will object, because there is no governmental involvement, and there is nothing more American than bringing one's own case into court. The proposal here fits into a whole class of litigation which has come to be part of our culture. There has never been a labor law proposal so easy to explain or defend.

This is not to say the amendment of the Civil Rights Act will make it impossible for an employer to resist organizing. But the employees who support the drive no longer have to hide. They no longer have to whisper in the dark. They can announce themselves and come out into the open. And it would be a profoundly serious risk for an employer to fire or even demote such an employee who puts on a union button, as it would place itself at risk of a lawsuit in federal court, with the employer subject to discovery, jury trials, injunctions, and legal fees that no employer trying to stomp out a union organizing drive has ever had to face before.

Would the Employees Win These Cases?

Some may object that many federal judges are conservative, and therefore would not rule in favor of employees. Civil rights lawyers groan that it is hard to win race and sex discrimination cases. But the impact of this law does not depend on winning outright. Virtually all of these cases settle. The great achievement of the civil rights laws to date has been to impose unacceptable costs on employers that engage in direct or overt discrimination—just the kind that labor organizers most want to stop. In particular, no employer with a real anti-union agenda would want to subject itself to wide-open discovery of its books and records (and contracts and contacts with union busters) in the middle of a highly political organizing campaign. With respect to overt discrimination, cases under the civil rights laws are easy to win. It is just that fact that has resulted in a world where most discrimination is subtler and less overt—and subtlety is not much help in stopping a union organizing drive. When employers discriminate on race or sex, they do not typically mean to "send a message," to say, "Hey, I discriminate, so back off." The kind of discrimination actionable now is typically not conscious—there is no claim of "intent," but simply disparate impact on minorities and women of a neutral rule. But an employer getting rid of pro-union organizers is very much trying to send a message to the other workers. The whole point is to make it clear even to the dullest imagination that the employer will come after you if you try to form a union. When we get to the point where employers are concealing anti-union animus in such cases and engage only in subtle discrimination, I believe we will be living in a different world, where union representation is the norm. We will not get there through legal victories in an old fashioned sense, but rather through a thousand notices of depositions that the business culture of the country changes.

How Will It Change the Labor Movement?

Workers today depend on union bureaucracies in Washington, D.C., to fight their battles—only the unions have the clout to get the attention of a federal agency like the NLRB, with its scarce resources for enforcing the laws. Since there are no legal fee awards in such cases today, only unions through a compulsory dues system can come up with the financial resources to fight for the legal rights of workers to organize. But if labor law "merges" with employment law, as the authors propose, all of this changes. Employees can get their own lawyers. They can control their own cases. And, instead of relying on union bureaucracies that have to husband their own resources, they can employ lawyers who are quite capable of recovering some or all of their legal fees. Civil rights laws allow for award of attorney's fees, so, in effect, employers that attempt to bust unions would end up "funding" the labor movement.

To sum up: so long as labor law inherited from the 1930s insulates employers from legal fees and discovery, it also insulates employers from the kind of law that has changed the whole culture with regard to race, sex, disability, age, and other forms of discrimination. The proposal here would change the culture just as much as the civil rights revolution did for these types of discrimination. And it would not only change the culture of employers, but of unions as well. It would give ordinary working Americans the chance to take the initiative to bring economic justice to this country and not depend on a weakened organized labor with limited resources to fight the global multinationals of our day.

Now read on. Sometimes a book can change the world.

—Thomas Geoghegan

Acknowledgments

The authors would like to thank Nathan Blevins for his excellent support as a Century Foundation research intern. Halley Potter, a policy associate at The Century Foundation also provided important supplementary research aid. The authors also would like to thank Joseph Cohen, David Madland, Mike Healey, Marty Malin, Danielle Marvit, César Rosado Marzán, Janice Pintar, Damon Silvers, and Emily Town for their discussions, advice, comments (sometimes critical), or review of previous drafts of the book.

CHAPTER ONE

Introduction

On April 4, 1968, when Dr. Martin Luther King Jr. was tragically gunned down in Memphis, Tennessee, he stood at the intersection of two great forces for enhancing human dignity: the civil rights movement, and the labor movement. King was in Memphis, it should be remembered, to support striking black sanitation workers, who marched with King carrying posters with the iconic message, "I AM A MAN."[1]

The signs had resonance in part because as black Americans, the sanitation workers were sick of being derisively referred to by racist whites as "boy." But in addition, as garbage collectors, they were tired of being poorly treated by management and by fellow citizens who looked down upon them. Because their employer would not provide them with a place to shower after work, garbage collectors were shunned by bus drivers and fellow passengers and often had to walk home. Managers, failing to fully recognize the basic humanity of sanitation workers, refused to install safety features on garbage trucks. After two sanitation workers were accidentally crushed to death by a defective packing mechanism on a garbage truck, 1,300 workers went on strike. Their message, "I AM A MAN," contained a powerful demand for better treatment.[2]

King rallied with sanitation workers and affirmed their dual message of racial and economic justice. "Whenever you are engaged in work that serves humanity and is for the building of humanity, it has dignity and it has worth," King told American Federation of State, County and Municipal Employees (AFSCME) workers in March 1968. He told them, "All labor has dignity."[3]

King had long seen the connection between the labor and civil rights movements as engines for human equality for men and women alike. While some racist union locals famously resisted progress for blacks, most were far more progressive on issues of civil rights than society as a whole. The massive labor federation, the American Federation of Labor and Congress of Industrial Organizations (AFL-CIO), became a critical supporter of civil rights legislation, including the 1964 Civil Rights Act, which, in Title VII, forbade racial discrimination in employment. In a 1961 speech to the AFL-CIO, King declared, "Our needs are identical with labor's needs: decent wages, fair working conditions, livable housing, old age security, health and welfare measures, conditions in which families can grow, have education for their children, and respect in the community. . . . The duality of interests of labor and Negroes makes any crisis which lacerates you, a crisis from which we bleed."[4] King also recognized that the region of the country most hostile to civil rights was also the most opposed to organized labor.[5] In the last year of his life, King had begun a multi-racial Poor People's Campaign, and in his final Sunday sermon, delivered at the National Cathedral in Washington, D.C., he called his vision of economic justice nothing less than his "last, greatest dream."[6] In Memphis, King recounted the great victories for civil rights, in Montgomery and Selma, and suggested, "You are going beyond purely civil rights questions to questions of human rights," raising "the economic issue." People must not only have the right to sit at a lunch counter, but also the right to afford a hamburger, he told the audience.[7]

In the years since King was struck down, enormous improvements have been made in racial attitudes and in the life chances of African Americans. The black middle-class has grown significantly, the number of black professionals has increased, and the black/white educational gap on such matters as high school graduation rates has shrunk dramatically.[8] While far more progress needs to be made, we have since 1968 witnessed a sea change in racial attitudes, culminating in the once-inconceivable idea of a black American president being elected. As Harvard Law professor Randall Kennedy has written, "One of the great achievements of the Civil Rights Revolution was its delegitimization of racial prejudice."[9] In that sense, the 1964 Civil Rights Act has proven a tremendous success. Among the broader public in America and internationally, the civil rights movement is rightly regarded as iconic in the struggle for human dignity and inclusion.[10] While more work surely needs to be done, the trajectory on race is generally pointed in the right direction.

By contrast, since the 1960s, the American labor movement has seen enormous setbacks. Labor once dreamed that, with the vanquishing of Jim Crow, the racism that had kept working-class whites in the South from uniting with blacks would diminish, and Southern states could be unionized. But organized labor did not conquer the South; instead, to a significant degree, Southern anti-union practices have spread through much of the country. From its peak in the mid-1950s, labor has declined from more than one-third of private sector workers (and one-half of the industrial workforce) to less than one-tenth.[11] Today, even public sector unionism is under attack in several states. Meanwhile, economic inequality has skyrocketed to the point that the top 1 percent of Americans own more than the bottom 90 percent, and income from productivity gains have gone almost exclusively to the top 10 percent.[12] Economists agree the two phenomena are connected, and that rising economic inequality in America is due in some significant measure to the weakness of the American labor movement.[13]

There are many factors that help explain why the nation has progressed on King's vision for civil rights while it has moved backward on his emphasis on the importance of economic equality and union strength. However, among the most important—and the easiest to remedy—is the substantial difference between the strength of our laws on civil rights and labor. Seventy-five years of experience with the National Labor Relations Act of 1935 (NLRA) and forty-five years of experience with Title VII of the Civil Rights Act of 1964 suggest that the former has proven largely ineffectual in protecting workers, while the latter has been quite successful in diminishing discrimination and changing social attitudes.

The 1964 Civil Rights Act, which was subsequently amended in 1991, provides powerful penalties for employers who discriminate on the basis of race, sex, national origin, or religion. Under the 1991 amendments, employment discrimination remedies have been expanded to include not only back pay but compensatory and punitive damages up to $300,000. Civil rights laws also provide plaintiffs with the opportunity to pursue legal discovery, something that employers assiduously seek to avoid. Furthermore, plaintiffs are given access to jury trials; and when plaintiffs prevail, defendants are liable for up to double the hourly rate for plaintiffs' attorneys' fees.[14]

Under the NLRA, it is likewise illegal to discriminate against employees for trying to organize a union, because lawmakers recognized that firms should not be allowed to use their disproportionate power to intimidate workers. But the penalties and processes under the NLRA are far weaker. If employers are found to have violated the law, they must reinstate any terminated employees and provide them with back pay, normally after a lengthy and arduous process of enforcement. And under the NLRA, there is extremely limited opportunity for discovery and no jury trial. Faced with the prospect of having to negotiate substantial wage and benefit increases with a union, businesses have a strong financial incentive to fire organizing employees and risk paying the penalties as a cost of doing business. Labor lawyer Thomas Geoghegan writes: "An employer who didn't break the law would have to be what economists call an 'irrational firm.'"[15]

The central thesis of this book is that the Civil Rights Act should be amended to add protection for employees seeking to organize a union. Just as it is illegal to fire someone for race or gender or national origin or religion, it would be illegal under the Civil Rights Act to fire someone for trying to organize or join a union.

Conceptually, the amendment would not break new ground, as it is already illegal to fire someone for organizing under the NLRA. But amending the Civil Rights Act to protect union organizing would offer two fundamental advantages. First, it would put teeth into the existing NLRA prohibition by applying the full force of Civil Rights penalties and procedures to businesses which break the law. Today, labor leaders note, the right to form a union is "the only legally guaranteed right that Americans are afraid to exercise."[16] Amending the Civil Rights Act would provide a far more effective deterrent to lawbreaking than the current statute and would recognize the theoretical right to organize as authentic.

The second advantage to this approach lies in its potential to break a longstanding political logjam surrounding labor law reform. Amending the Civil Rights Act rather than the NLRA would, for the broader American public, help elevate the debate from the obscure confines of labor law to the higher arena of civil rights, which Americans readily understand. Whereas labor law is seen by many as a body of technical rules governing relations between two sets of "special interests"—business and labor— Americans understand the principle of nondiscrimination as an issue of fundamental fairness. Employment rights have long been considered civil rights, and there is no reason to exclude labor rights from this formulation. Framing labor organizing as a civil right could provide a new paradigm that might fundamentally alter the political landscape, breaking the deadlock over reform.

Since the passage of the anti-labor Labor–Management Relations Act in the 1940s (known as the Taft-Hartley Act), organized labor has had four major chances to reform labor laws in order to level the playing field for workers. Each time that Democrats have controlled the presidency and both houses in Congress they have sought to alter labor law, and each time they have failed. Under Lyndon Johnson, Democrats fell short in a Senate effort to modify Taft-Hartley. Under Jimmy Carter, labor law reform that would have enhanced penalties for unfair labor practices failed by two votes in a Democratically controlled Senate. During Bill Clinton's first term, legislation to outlaw the permanent replacement of strikers stalled. And under Barack Obama, the Employee Free Choice Act (EFCA) to stiffen penalties for employer abuses and allow a majority of employees to authorize union representation through "card check" procedures was not even put to a formal vote in the Senate.[17]

The fundamental problem with these efforts is that labor is caught in a political box. In order to achieve reform, labor needs political power, which requires expanding union membership; but in order to grow, unions need labor law reform. As Harvard Law Professor Paul C. Weiler noted more than a decade ago, "No part of American law in the last 50 years has been less amenable to reform than labor law."[18] The Civil Rights strategy would offer a fresh approach. Republican-controlled bodies of Congress are unlikely to support efforts to strengthen labor under any circumstances, but progressives need to begin developing a new strategy now so that when they do regain full political power, they do not miss a fifth chance to revitalize labor.

Recent developments suggest that labor may have the public on its side. Following the 2010 elections, Republican governors in Wisconsin, Ohio, Indiana, and elsewhere took what had primarily been an assault on private sector collective bargaining rights to the public sector, which had previously faced a more favorable climate. These attacks on public sector collective bargaining prominently raised fundamental issues about the role of labor in American society and energized many progressives who had taken the right of employees to band together collectively for granted. Indeed, recent polling suggests that while the opinions of Americans are mixed on unions, they strongly believe, by margins of two to one, and even three to one, in the basic right of collective bargaining.[19] In November 2011, the people of Ohio overwhelmingly voted to repeal an anti-union law that restricted public employee collective bargaining rights.

Moreover, the attack on public sector unions for receiving more generous pension and health benefits than private sector workers raises the possibility of a different discussion: rather than pursuing a race to the bottom, where the diminishing benefits of nonunionized private employees are used as a club against unionized public employees, why not take steps to strengthen private sector unionization, so that private sector employees can enjoy the same level of benefits as those enjoyed by those employed in the public sector?

A Brief Overview

The argument for conceiving of labor organizing as a civil right proceeds in six chapters. Chapter 2 outlines the history of the importance of the American labor movement and explains what is at stake in resurrecting unions. In the modern history of the United States, organized labor has had an enormous impact on building the American middle class, which is why labor's subsequent collapse has had such dire consequences.

Bargaining by unions gives workers a larger slice of the economic pie, in the form of higher wages and benefits. Research finds that union wages are 28 percent higher than nonunion wages overall; that even controlling for occupation, education levels, and other factors, union wages are 15 percent higher; and that union members are much more likely to have employer health care plans than nonunion workers. But unions do not just boost their own members' wages and benefits. There is also a positive "spillover" effect of unions, whereby nonunionized employees see increased wages as nonunion employers compete with union firms to attract workers.[20]

As a result, during labor's heyday, after World War II, America enjoyed broadly shared economic growth, and saw the emergence of what journalist George Packer calls a "middle-class democracy."[21] In the period from 1947 to 1977, workers in the bottom fifth saw pay increase by 116 percent, even faster than those in the top fifth (who saw pay increase by 99 percent).[22]

Likewise, during their years of strength following World War II, unions helped increase political participation among workers and used their muscle to pass landmark legislation for Medicare and civil rights. In a country with lots of different interest groups, labor stands out above all others on the liberal side.[23] Conservatives fully understood this. Passage of the anti-labor Taft-Hartley legislation in the 1940s was specifically targeted at breaking what appeared to be the possibility of a permanent Democratic majority.[24] Ronald Reagan's attack on unionized air traffic controllers in the 1980s was part of a concerted effort to damage labor, and the current Republican assault on public sector unions has similarly been advanced as a way of fundamentally changing the politics of key swing states in this country.[25]

The cumulative effect of these attacks has been considerable, as private sector labor unions in particular have been considerably weakened. The effects on our politics and our economy have been devastating. In the thirty years from 1977 to 2007, during labor's precipitous decline, America witnessed what former Labor Secretary Robert Reich calls the Middle-Class Squeeze.[26]

The evidence linking declining union density and increasing economic inequality is strengthened by a comparison of the U.S. experience with that of other countries. Labor has seen some drop off in other nations, but not nearly as much as in the United States, and evidence suggests countries with higher levels of union density tend to have substantially lower degrees of economic inequality.

Although some suggest we should not be concerned about unequal economic results, only unequal opportunity, the two are inextricably linked: huge gaps between rich and poor have reduced social mobility. The shrinking middle class also threatens the integrity of our democracy and weakens the consumer demand that drives economic growth.[27]

Chapter 3 looks at possible reasons for labor's decline. The contention that changes in the economy and economic globalization inevitably mean weak unions is belied by the strong union movements in many rich countries. Likewise, the notion that modern workers no longer desire to join unions is contradicted by evidence suggesting that 53 percent of non-managerial, nonunion workers would probably or definitely vote for a union if they could in 2007—up from 30 percent in 1984. If just one-quarter of those people unionized, the labor movement would double in size.[28]

Instead, the social science evidence fundamentally suggests that the NLRA has failed to deter employers from firing workers who are trying to organize a union. The chief problem: while existing labor law makes it technically illegal to fire employees for trying to organize, the price for violating the law is extremely small, leading employers to break the law with increasing frequency. In 2005, the National Labor Relations Board awarded back pay to more than 30,000 Americans who were illegally fired or otherwise disciplined for trying to organize a union—up from less than 1,000 in the 1950s.[29] Cornell University researcher Kate Bronfenbrenner found that, between 1999 and 2003, employees were illegally dismissed in 34 percent of union drives for engaging in union organizing.[30] A 2007 study by the Center for Economic and Policy Research estimates that "almost one in five union organizers or activists can expect to be fired as a result of their activities in union election campaigns."[31]

The NLRB arbitration process for reinstating wrongfully discharged employees is also lengthy and laborious. In fiscal year 2009, in instances where the NLRB reached a decision following the issuance of an unfair labor practice complaint, it took a median of 483 days for the decision to be reached.[32] Meanwhile, the average amount of back pay awarded for an unfair labor practice was just $5,149.[33]

One exception to the general decline in labor is the increase in union density among public sector workers, where state statutes rather than the NLRA govern union elections and more than one-third of workers are organized. The fact that public sector unionization has grown in the past half-century while private sector union representation has plummeted suggests that the threat of termination may be a significant deterrent to successful organizing efforts. As journalist Hendrik Hertzberg has written in the *New Yorker:* "It's not that toll-booth attendants, clerks in government bureaucracies and schoolteachers are by nature tough, hardened militants or have bulging, ropy forearms. It's that their employer, the government, is in a poor position to routinely and brazenly flout the plain language of the law."[34]

Likewise, Chapter 3 explores the contrast between unionization under the NLRA and the Railway Labor Act (RLA). Under the RLA, an employee who is terminated during an organization drive can seek an immediate injunction in federal court and be reinstated within days, making employers' firing of union organizers rare in industries covered by the RLA. Not surprisingly, the union density of workers under the RLA is significantly higher than under the NLRA. Between 1955 and 1997 private sector union density declined from 33 percent to 9.8 percent, while union density of railway employees increased during that same time period to reach levels between 80 percent and 85 percent, and the density of unionized airline employees increased to 65 percent.[35] Union density has declined some in recent years even under the RLA with the growth of thrift airlines like JetBlue, but it remains far higher than under the NLRA. In a recent year, union density in the rail transportation industry was 71 percent, and the union density in the air transportation industry was 49 percent.[36]

Of course, the issue of labor law reform is complex, and disciplining and firing employees who try to organize a union is not the only way that employers seek to kill collective bargaining drives. Firms also threaten to (and do) close plants, permanently replace striking workers, and fail to bargain in good faith when unions are certified, among other things. But providing genuine punishment for wrongful terminations, harassment, threats, and the like would be a simple and important step forward in leveling the playing field by disabling a key weapon businesses use to intimidate workers. As Patricia Greenfield of the National Labor College has noted, "A few well-placed firings, even if they're illegal, can stop a union campaign in its tracks."[37]

Chapter 4 takes a look at the international landscape and finds that the United States is an outlier among advanced industrial nations in failing to protect worker rights. Under international law, the right of workers to organize is considered a core democratic value. Article 23 of the Universal Declaration of Human Rights—which the United States took the lead in pushing—provides, "Everyone has the right to form and to join trade unions for the protection of his interests."[38]

Yet among advanced industrial democracies, the United States does a very poor job of protecting labor rights. In a 2010 report, Freedom House finds that the United States is less free than forty-one other nations in protecting labor rights. The report declared, "The United States is almost alone among economically advanced democracies in its lack of a strong trade union movement in the private sector," and cited weak penalties for illegal worker discharges as among the causes. Freedom House and other researchers find that our major European competitors—such as Germany, France, and the United Kingdom—protect labor rights far more effectively than the United States.[39] In contrast to the low ranking of the United States in protecting labor rights, Freedom House commended the United States for the strength of its civil rights laws.[40]

Chapter 5 outlines the specific ways in which the Civil Rights Act would be amended to include protection for workers trying to organize and examines some of the implications. Title VII of the 1964 Civil Rights Act (which now prohibits discrimination based on race, gender, religion, and other factors from wrongful termination and other forms of employment discrimination) would be amended to prohibit discrimination against workers who are attempting to organize a labor union, making them eligible not only for back pay but for compensatory and punitive damages as well.

Significantly, Title VII remedies for unlawful discharge of unionizing workers would likely be an even more effective deterrent than they have been for racial and gender discrimination because unlawfully discharged workers trying to form a union would have an important financial reservoir not available to victims of race and gender bias. American labor unions had an estimated income of $16 billion in 2010.[41] By contrast, civil rights and women's organizations have much smaller financial bases on which to draw, so most women and people of color must rely on contingency lawyers.

Conceivably, writing labor organizing protections into the Civil Rights Act could also spawn a cultural shift in employer behavior. Employers who are found guilty of racial or gender discrimination are today seen to have done something shameful, a seismic shift from the days when business routinely espoused racist and chauvinistic attitudes. Today, there is no lucrative industry to aid employers in thwarting civil rights laws as there is to keep unions out. Instead, the opposite is found, where employers spend billions of dollars a year on human resource departments in part to ensure that all employees understand the requirements of Title VII.[42]

By contrast, managers are unapologetic about wanting to silence the voice of workers. Wal-Mart CEO Lee Scott, for example, famously said, "We like driving the car and we're not going to give the steering wheel to anybody but us."[43] Shifting labor organizing protections to civil rights legislation could, over time, bring about a cultural shift in which the country sees corporations that fire employees for trying to form a union, join the middle class, and have a say in the workplace, as morally suspect—as they already are seen in Europe.

In chapter 5, we address three additional sets of issues concerning how labor rights could be administered and resolved under the Civil Rights Act. First, we argue that the broader coverage of the Civil Rights Act (to include public employees, agricultural laborers, and supervisors) makes sense with respect to union organizing because the NLRA's exclusion of these groups was based on a 1930s understanding of the American workforce that no longer promotes the purposes of the act. Second, we argue that for labor suits under the Civil Rights Act, procedures similar to those of the Equal Employment Opportunity Commission (EEOC) should be followed, but the NLRB should continue to administer disputes. This approach would combine a process that has proved effective with an agency that is finely attuned to the nuances of labor law through its more than seventy-five years of experience handling labor disputes. Third, the chapter argues that an employee should be able to sue both for the right to join a union or not to join a union. Just as the Civil Rights Act extends both to minority and to majority groups, similarly, it should protect the individual employee from employer reprisals for his decisions on joining or not joining a union. In practice, employers would be unlikely to discriminate against employees for failing to join a union, but as an individual right, respect for it should be symmetrical. The amended Civil Rights Act would preserve the ability of unions to require non-union employees to nevertheless pay an agency fee to avoid "free riding."

In chapter 6, we address the connection between the labor and civil rights movements in the United States and explain why the Civil Rights Act is the right vehicle for protecting those trying to organize a union, for three distinct reasons: (1) labor organizing is a basic human right, which is bound up with an important democratic right to association; (2) strengthening labor advances the values and interests of the Civil Rights movement by promoting dignity and equality, particularly for people of color; (3) and stronger unions can enhance existing protections against discrimination by race, gender, national origin, and religion by reducing employer discretion and enhancing processes for redress.

Labor organizing is connected to the fundamental constitutional right of association that is recognized as part of the First Amendment.[44] In a democracy, individuals have a right to join together with others to promote their interests and values. Just as the original Civil Rights Act extended the Fourteenth Amendment's prohibition against government discrimination to apply to private sector employers, adding anti-discrimination protection for labor organizing extends a First Amendment right against government restraint of free association to apply to private sector employers. Of course, Congress already extended association rights to the private sector when it passed the 1935 NLRA recognizing the "right to self-organization." Including labor protections in the Civil Rights Act, therefore, does not break new ground conceptually, but it does provide workers with a much better way to hold accountable employers who violate their rights.

Some people believe that civil rights laws should only protect individuals from discrimination based on immutable factors such as race, national origin, and gender. But civil rights legislation has long gone beyond that to prohibit discrimination based on behavioral factors such as pregnancy, prior criminal conviction, whistle-blowing, indebtedness, or bankruptcy.[45] The 1964 act itself included protection against discrimination based on religion, which is a mutable characteristic. A Christian who converts to Islam, for example, is protected against an employer's religious discrimination; the employer cannot defend discrimination on the basis that the employee chose to convert.

Significantly, anti-discrimination laws apply even when they could hurt the profitability of a company. In the early days of civil rights law, for example, law firms were not allowed to justify discrimination against black attorneys based on evidence that white clients would not want to work with them. The principle already established under the NLRA and UN Declaration of Human Rights suggests that, even if unions cut into corporate profits, employers cannot abuse their economic power by firing employees for trying to organize.

Moreover, strengthening labor can advance the larger objectives of the Civil Rights Act itself: promoting greater dignity and equality, particularly for people of color. The labor and civil rights movements, while not always allied, are fundamentally bound by similar values, interests, tactics, and enemies. Labor recognizes that individuals should be treated with decency, a core belief of the civil rights movement; their emphasis on a shared humanity explains why labor leaders and civil rights advocates refer to one another as brothers and sisters.

Not only do the movements share similar values, King recognized that they have common interests. As a predominantly working people, blacks had much to gain from a stronger union movement. Julian Bond, as chairman of the National Association for the Advancement of Colored People (NAACP), noted in a 2005 address that minorities are disproportionately represented in organized labor; that African Americans who are members of unions earn 35 percent more than nonunionized black people; and that black Americans are more likely than whites to want to join unions.[46] In this way, amending the Civil Rights Act to protect workers trying to organize a union would not diminish the act's commitment to racial equality; it would extend and affirm that commitment in new ways.

The civil rights and labor movements have also used similar tactics, like civil disobedience, sit-ins, and picket lines. And both movements faced a common source of resistance. It is no accident that the eleven states that today are most resistant to unions and have the lowest union density rates are all states that were previously governed by Jim Crow.[47]

Historical evidence is clear that the anti-union "right to work" movement was originally aimed at weakening labor's ability to fight against racial segregation.[48]

Finally, stronger unions, by protecting employees against arbitrary dismissals in general, provide an additional shield against the type of racial and gender discrimination that is forbidden by the Civil Rights Act. Most employees currently work "at-will": they can be fired for "good cause, bad cause, or no cause." Unions work to remove arbitrary terminations and the at-will employment system from the workplace, and limit the type of employer discretion that allows discrimination to take place. Unions also put procedures in place to address grievances, providing an employee with the possibility of faster relief should she suffer from discrimination. In this way, adding the right to organize to the Civil Rights Act does not distract from the original focus of the act, but rather enhances it through internal nongovernmental procedures that can remedy racial discrimination in the workplace in a faster and more efficient manner than litigation.

Chapter 7 concludes the book with a consideration of the political advantages to framing the right to organize as a matter of moral values rather than a battle of raw "interests," (labor versus management); and the advantages of having a fight over "anti-discrimination law" rather than "labor law."

Politically, thinking of labor organizing as a civil right instead of as a part of labor law takes the focus off of "unions," which some Americans disfavor, and on to an egregious practice of employers: firing people for reasons having nothing to do with job performance. In the battle over the Employee Free Choice Act in 2009, unions tried to highlight the basic unfairness of dismissals for union organizing, while business interests tried to highlight the bill's use of "card check" rather than the secret ballot. Corporate America used the secret ballot issue to feed into ugly stereotypes suggesting that union thugs would coerce workers into supporting organized labor. And the complexity of the law allowed employers to mischaracterize the legislation.

Business will oppose any effort to give labor a level playing field, but by avoiding the secret ballot issue—and focusing directly on illegal dismissals—amending the Civil Rights Act to protect labor organizing maximizes the political advantages. If Americans are somewhat ambivalent about organized labor per se, the antidiscrimination principle in employment is very firmly rooted. In the late 1990s, for example, 59 percent of

Americans continued to believe "homosexual behavior is wrong" yet a phenomenal 84 percent said gays should "have equal rights in terms of job opportunities."[49] There is an enormous political benefit to shifting the question from whether people like labor unions or not to the issue of the discriminatory behavior of employers.

More generally, the rhetoric of "rights" is very powerful in American political discourse. Indeed, when asked to identify government's most important role, 59 percent say it is to protect individual rights and liberty.[50] Ironically, for years business has appropriated the slogan "right to work" to signify state legislation that allows employees to benefit from collective bargaining agreements without paying their fair share of dues. Although some advocates of unions may object to an emphasis on individual rights over group solidarity, at the early stages of a union organizing campaign, individuals do need protection so they can later assert collective demands. Acknowledging this, some union leaders are beginning to take back the rhetoric of rights, and the AFL-CIO has sponsored rallies to protest illegal firings, likening the campaign "to a new civil rights movement."[51] Connecting labor to the civil rights movement is especially vital to making the issue easier to understand for young people, who may not personally know any friends or family members who are part of organized labor.

Labor law has become increasingly complex and technical, and is understood by few beyond its practitioners. As a civil right, labor law becomes almost intuitively understandable and its importance becomes easy to communicate to those outside the field. Whereas labor law reform does not excite people, civil rights does. Thomas Geoghegan writes: "If we only thought of the [NLRA] as a civil rights law, instead of a labor law, then maybe liberals would wake up and do something."[52]

Americans long to be part of something larger than themselves, and just as promoters of equal educational opportunity and a cleaner environment have characterized their causes as part of this generation's civil rights movement, so labor organizing—which shares with the civil rights movement the basic quest for human dignity—has a very strong claim to that mantle. In Memphis, Martin Luther King Jr. understood that the fate of the labor movement and the civil rights community were inextricably bound. As we shall argue through this book, now is the time to write the protection of organized labor into the Civil Rights Act itself.

CHAPTER TWO

Why the Collapse of the American Labor Movement Matters

The rise of the American organized labor movement after the New Deal ushered in an era of broadly shared prosperity and progressive political action from the 1940s through the 1970s. The slow collapse of American unions in the subsequent decades—particularly in private sector industries that are governed by the National Labor Relations Act (NLRA)—has brought with it skyrocketing economic inequality, a shrinking middle class, and political gridlock on progressive legislation. While there have been many factors contributing to growing economic inequality—including globalization and structural changes in the economy that put a greater premium on education—it cannot be denied that the historic decline in organized labor has had an enormous impact on the economic and political landscape of the country.

We begin this chapter by examining the ways in which labor has promoted a vibrant American middle-class democracy. We then turn to an analysis of labor's decline and its effects on the ability of workers to receive a fair share of the economic pie, as well as the ability of progressives to pass social legislation. We next take a look abroad and consider the correlation between unionization rates and economic inequality across the world. We conclude with a discussion of why inequality matters and why all Americans, whether or not they are themselves union members, should be deeply concerned about the decimation of organized labor in this country.

The Contribution of Organized Labor
to Shared Prosperity and Social Progress

With the onset of the industrial revolution in America, workers recognized that they could not, as individuals, negotiate a fair wage and decent working conditions, but if they organized, their collective strength could begin to match that of their employer. The Knights of Labor, founded by skilled workers in 1869, engaged in mass organizing of unskilled labor, but collapsed in 1886, to be replaced by the American Federation of Labor, a collection of craft unions. In the years that followed, labor organization began to gain acceptance among workers, and the percentage of nonagricultural workers who were union members rose from 1.8 percent in 1880 to 7.5 percent by 1900. Throughout this period and through the 1920s, employers saw labor organization as a serious threat and fought back, going so far as to hire private armies to suppress striking workers. The efforts of employers were aided by courts, which issued injunctions against strikers. At this point, union organizing flat-lined, so that by 1928, union membership remained below 10 percent of the nonagricultural workforce.[1]

Labor union membership once again soared, however, after passage of New Deal legislation to strengthen unions. These new laws included the Norris-LaGuardia Act of 1932, which barred federal courts from issuing injunctions against nonviolent strikes, and the National Labor Relations Act of 1935, which established the affirmative right to organize. By 1939, the proportion of nonagricultural workers who were union members reached 28.6 percent, a figure that grew to more than one-third—34.7 percent—of nonagricultural workers by 1954, an all-time high in the United States. (Among industrial workers, the rate was 50 percent.) After that, the union density rate began a slow decline, but remained above one-quarter of nonagricultural workers in 1972, and did not fall below 20 percent until 1983.[2] The strength of labor during its heyday, particularly between 1947 and 1977, was significant in the life of the nation, as we explain below, because labor truly helped build a modern middle-class democracy in America.

The Economic Impact of Unions: Building a Middle-Class

In the economic sphere, unions bolstered—and continue to this day to contribute to—broadly shared prosperity in three main ways. First, workers in unionized occupations tend to garner a larger proportion of a firm's earnings for workers than in nonunionized occupations, where shareholders and management hold disproportionate bargaining power. According to the Bureau of Labor Statistics, in 2010, among full-time wage and salary workers, union members had median weekly earnings of $908, while those who were not represented by unions had median weekly earnings of $710 (a 28 percent difference).[3] This finding probably overstates the union wage premium because unionized workers tend to have higher levels of education and work in higher paying industries than nonunion workers, but even after controlling for a number of factors, such as age, education level, gender, and industry, union hourly wages are about 15 percent higher than nonunion wages, according to the Center for Economic and Policy Research.[4]

By keeping pressure on firms to provide workers with a greater share of the increased earnings from productivity gains, unions have been found to compress the wage differences between management and labor. According to one study, "controlling for variation in human resource practices, unionized establishments have on average a 23.2 percentage point lower manager-to-worker pay ratio relative to non-union workplaces."[5]

Second, unions bargain for better worker benefits, including health care and pension plans, than would otherwise be provided. According to the Bureau of Labor Statistics, 92 percent of union workers have access to retirement benefits, compared with 65 percent of nonunion workers. Likewise, 93 percent of union workers get health benefits, compared with 70 percent of nonunion workers. Some 84 percent of union workers get life insurance coverage, compared with 58 percent of nonunion workers. And 83 percent of union workers get some form of paid sick leave, compared with 64 percent of nonunion workers. [6]

Union employees tend not only to have better rates of coverage, but also more generous benefits. In the health care arena, for example, non-unionized employees have to pay nearly double the share of their single-coverage health insurance premium compared to unionized employees. Nonunion employees pay, on average, 19 percent of the cost of their individual health insurance premiums, compared to 10 percent for unionized employees, according to the Bureau of Labor Statistics. For family coverage, the gap between premium payments is even larger, with non-union employees paying 33 percent of premium costs, compared with 18 percent for unionized employees.[7] Moreover, according to Lawrence Mishel and Matthew Walters of the Economic Policy Institute, union health care deductibles are, on average, 18 percent lower than nonunion insurance plans. In terms of retirement security, employers, on average, pay for 72 percent of union pensions, compared to just 44 percent for nonunionized workers. [8]

Third, unions strengthen the middle class by benefiting nonunionized workers whose employers compete with unionized employers for talent. Improvement in union wages and benefits have been found to "spill over" into nonunionized firms as nonunion employers boost wages and benefits to keep unions out and vie with unionized employers for the best employees. Economist Yu Hsing's 2010 analysis in *Applied Economic Letters,* for example, finds "a one percentage point increase in union wages is expected to raise nonunion wages by 0.102 percentage points in the long run."[9] At large firms, the spillover effect can be as high as 10–20 percent.[10] Because the number of nonunionized workers in the United States is so much larger than unionized workers, Princeton University's Henry Farber has calculated that the total combined value of the wage increase for nonunion workers due to unions is almost as large as for unionized workers.[11] Importantly, some research finds that spillover effects are stronger when union density is high.[12]

In the era when unions remained fairly strong—1947 to 1977—America enjoyed what Robert Reich calls "The Great Prosperity," a thirty-year period when "everyone's wages grew—not just those at the top." The pay of the bottom fifth grew at a slightly higher rate than the top fifth, and median wages more than doubled, from about $25,000 to $55,000 (expressed in 2007 dollars). These years also saw the rise of a new social compact, in which employers provided substantial health care and pension benefits, as well as paid vacation time and weekends off, all practices that first originated in unionized firms.[13]

The Political Impact of Unions
in Softening the Sharp Edges of Markets

Labor also helped change the political landscape of America during the 1940s through the 1970s for a number of reasons. For one thing, labor unions helped create a culture of participation among workers. The give-and-take of collective bargaining, being involved in workplace decision-making, and the process of voting on union contracts and for union leadership have been called crucial drivers of "democratic acculturation."[14] In addition, union members routinely would staff phone banks and go door to door to encourage other members and like-minded citizens to go out to vote on Election Day—a practice that continues to this day. In the last two weeks of the 2008 campaign, for example, the AFL-CIO mobilized 250,000 volunteers in twenty battleground states.[15] In 2010, the AFL-CIO said 200,000 union members volunteered, canvassing 8.5 million households.[16] One study found that for every one-percentage-point increase in a state's union density, voter turnout increased by 0.2 to 0.25 percentage points. A ten-percentage-point increase in union density, in other words, could translate into 3 million more votes in a presidential election.[17] And these efforts appear to have an especially important effect on the voting behavior of working-class voters. In congressional districts where unions have special campaigns to increase political participation, working-class voters are just as likely to vote as others; in districts lacking those campaigns, working-class voters are ten percentage points less likely to vote than others.[18]

Organized labor can also serve as a crucial counterweight to business interests, representing what unions call "the people's lobby." In an environment where wealthy individuals and corporations exert an outsized influence, unions have been—and continue to be—a major source of funding for candidates concerned about the middle class. According to the Center for Responsive Politics, for the two-decade period extending from 1989 to 2010, six of the top ten, and twelve of the top twenty largest total donors were labor unions. Unions donated a combined total of roughly $380 million dollars, almost all of it to Democrats and progressive causes. No union gave more than 10 percent of total donations to Republicans or conservative causes.[19] In the 2010 elections, for example, the Center found that unions spent nearly $60 million, accounting for 62 percent of all outside spending on progressive issues.[20] Even within Democratic primaries, unions are often an important source of funding for candidates more in tune with middle-class interests.[21] The importance of unions as a funding source for progressives is likely to increase as a result of the Supreme Court's 2010 decision in *Citizens United v. Federal Election Commission*, allowing unlimited independent expenditures and donations to "Super PACs" by unions and corporations.[22]

In addition, union education campaigns can have a considerable impact on voting behavior. According to one study, union members are between 18 percent and 50 percent more likely to back union-endorsed candidates in an election.[23] In the 2010 elections for the House of Representatives, for example, *Washington Post* columnist Harold Meyerson writes that Democrats performed twenty-four points better among working-class whites in unionized households than in nonunionized households. While

white working-class voters in union households favored House Democrats by a margin of 55 percent to 43 percent, nonunion working-class
whites favored Republicans by a whopping 68 percent to 31 percent. The
twenty-four-point difference exists "not because unionized UPS drivers
and nonunion FedEx drivers, say, are two different species of human,"
he wrote. "It's because the unions' political education and mobilization
programs are very effective."[24]

For all these reasons, American labor has been central to the progressive cause, and during labor's heyday was in large measure responsible
for many of the major pieces of social legislation passed. From the 1930s
through the 1970s in particular, labor was a powerful force, even in what
are currently conservative states. In Indiana, for example, in the mid-
1960s, the legislature had more union officials than lawyers or lobbyists.[25]

In the 1930s, labor fought for the federal Fair Labor Standards
Act, which provided a minimum wage, and time-and-a-half for work
beyond a traditional forty-hour week.[26] Moreover, according to Jacob
Hacker of Yale and Paul Pierson of University of California–Berkeley,
"Unions were at the front lines of every major economic battle of the
mid-century—from the successful struggle for an expanded Social Security program in the 1950s to the passage of Medicare in 1965."[27] With
respect to anti-discrimination legislation, Missouri Democratic Con-
gressman Richard Bolling argued, "we would never have passed the Civil
Rights Act without labor. They had the muscle; the other civil rights
groups did not."[28] On the health care front, Jill Quadango of Florida
State University writes: "The AFL-CIO won Medicare by mobilizing its
extensive union network of state federations and local chapters, organizing a grassroots senior citizens' movement, and supporting Democratic
Party members who served on key congressional committees."[29] Considering the impact of American unions over time, Columbia historian Eric
Foner argues: "There is no real hope for progressive social change in this
country without a strong labor movement."[30]

Conservatives have long understood the importance of labor to the
progressive coalition, which helps explain why Republicans have con-
tinually sought legislation to weaken organized unions over the past several decades. Republicans knew, says labor lawyer Thomas Geoghegan,
that gains in labor organizing helped consolidate the New Deal coalition,
which is why, when the Republicans won a congressional majority in
the 1940s, they swiftly moved to pass Taft-Hartley to reign in unions by
restricting secondary boycotts and authorizing so-called "right to work"

state laws that allow nonunion members to benefit from collective bargaining agreements without paying dues. Geoghegan writes: "The Republicans, by the 1940s, were becoming frightened. With the CIO growing every year, America was threatening to become a one-party state. So if Republicans couldn't stop the CIO, and stop it soon, they could end up extinct, like the Federalists or the Whigs. Then, in 1946, the Republicans had a break," and were able, a year later, to pass Taft-Hartley.[31] Republicans fiercely fought pro-union labor law reform in the 1970s because the legislation, as teacher unionist Albert Shanker noted, could have changed "the entire politics of the Congress of the United States."[32]

In more recent years, the Republican assault on public sector unions in Wisconsin, Indiana, and Ohio is also testament to the political importance of labor. The attack is part of a larger effort "to bring us closer to a more permanent Republican majority," Indiana University political science professor Marjorie Hershey has argued.[33] *The New Republic*'s John Judis suggests that the political stakes in these public sector union fights are enormous. He writes: "For 20 years, if not longer, conservative Republicans have been lamenting the power of public unions to raise money and campaign for Democratic candidates. . . . Now, Republicans like [Wisconsin Governor Scott] Walker seem to believe that, if they can further defang the unions, they can permanently alter the country's political landscape. And here's the scary part: They're right." Labor is especially critical, given its importance in swing states that can sway presidential elections. Judis writes: "If Wisconsin and Ohio and similar states in the North eradicate public employee unions, it will certainly make it harder for Democrats to carry these crucial swing states. But it will also thwart the development of social liberalism in these states and, therefore, in the rest of the country."[34]

The Collapse of Organized Labor
in the United States and Its Fallout

The steady Republican attacks on organized labor over time had a devastating effect on union strength in the United States. As we shall discuss in chapter 3, standard explanations about the decline in unions—globalization and declining worker interest in unions—do not adequately explain labor's collapse. Conscious public policy decisions were more important. The effects of the 1947 Taft-Hartley Act, coupled with actions such as Ronald Reagan's decision to fire striking air traffic controllers in 1981, helped create a climate in which private sector union membership fell from more than one-third in the 1950s to 6.9 percent in 2010.[35] Individual private occupations in particular have seen steep fall offs. Construction declined from a 28 percent unionization rate in 1983 to 14.6 percent in 2010. Over the same period, manufacturing of durable goods saw union density drop from 29.2 percent to 10.3 percent, manufacturing in nondurable goods from 25.9 percent to 11.7 percent, mining from 20.6 percent to 8 percent, and retail from 8.6 percent to 4.8 percent.[36]

Significantly, there are a few bright spots for organized labor, where union density has increased or remained high, such as in the public sector and the rail and air transportation industry, neither of which is governed by the National Labor Relations Act (see further discussion in chapter 3). But these are the exceptions to the rule. When all workers, public and private, are taken together, the downward trajectory for labor is unmistakable. Looking at the past thirty years, combined public and private membership declined substantially, from 20.1 percent in 1983 to 11.8 percent in 2010.[37]

Rising Economic Inequality and a Shrinking Middle Class

During the very same period that labor has been declining, the United States has experienced large increases in inequality, as measured by both income and wealth. According to the 2011 report of the Congressional Budget Office (CBO), the average after-tax income (in inflation-adjusted dollars) for the wealthiest 1 percent of Americans increased 275 percent between 1979 and 2007. For others in the top quintile, the increase was 65 percent, but the middle three-fifths, income increased by just under 40 percent, and the bottom quintile by just 18 percent.[38] Census data released in September 2011 found that the average American family actually saw its income drop in the previous decade, "the first time that has happened in this country for at least five decades." During the same period, executive pay and corporate profits soared.[39] According to the Economic Policy Institute, chief executive officers of corporations earned twenty-four times as much as the average American worker in 1965, but that ratio soared to 243 to 1 in 2010.[40]

Expressed in terms of the percentage of income shared by various groups, the CBO's 2011 report found that the after-tax income of the top 1 percent more than doubled between 1979 and 2007, from nearly 8 percent to 17 percent. The most affluent quintile now has more after-tax income (53 percent) than the bottom 80 percent.[41] With household incomes skewing toward high and low extremes, economists have begun to refer to the "disappearing middle-class."

Meanwhile, wealth inequality, which has always been greater than income inequality, has deepened. According to Sylvia A. Allegretto of the Economic Policy Institute, from 1962 to 2009, the average household wealth of the top 20 percent of Americans (in real 2009 dollars) more than doubled from $773,000 to $1,711,500. For the remaining 80 percent, the increase was much more modest, rising from $45,500 to $62,900. The ratio of the median wealth of the richest 1 percent of Americans to the median wealth of all Americans skyrocketed in the same time period, rising from 125 to 1 in 1962 (for every $1 held by the median American family, the median family of the richest 1 percent had $125) to 225 to 1 in 2009.[42] Astonishingly, in 2007, the wealthiest 400 Americans had almost as much wealth as the 150 million Americans who comprise the bottom 50 percent of the American population.[43]

The stagnation of median income during these periods was not due to slow productivity gains. Labor was producing more for the economy, but garnered a smaller proportion of the total gains. According to Lawrence Mishel and Heidi Shierholz of the Economic Policy Institute, between 1980 and 2009, worker productivity in the United States grew by 80 percent, but real median wages only increased by 12 percent. The authors find that if labor had shared in these productivity gains as it had in the past when labor unions were stronger, median wages would be $31.98 an hour, 61 percent higher than the actual average real wage in 2009.[44]

Figure 2.1 from the Economic Policy Institute vividly illustrates the way in which wages and productivity rose together between 1947 and 1973 but then sharply diverged after that.

In fact, productivity gains benefited only the wealthiest Americans. Northwestern University researchers Ian Dew-Becker and Robert J. Gordon found, "Our most surprising result is that over the entire period 1966–2001, as well as over 1997–2001, only the top 10 percent of the income distribution enjoyed a growth rate of real wage and salary income equal to or above the average rate of economy-wide productivity growth."[45]

The timing of the decline in labor and the decline in the American middle class is striking. As the Center for American Progress's David Madland, Karla Walter, and Nick Bunker have found, between 1969 and 2009, each slip in the unionization rate was closely coupled with a fall in the proportion of income going to the middle three quintiles of the income distribution (see figure 2.2).

FIGURE 2.1
Growth of Productivity, Hourly Wages, and Hourly Compensation, 1947–2011

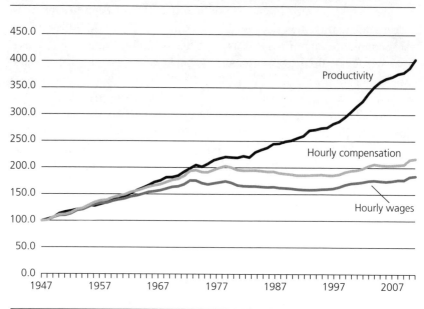

Source: Data provided to authors by Lawrence Mishel, Economic Policy Institute.

Madland and his colleagues' analysis also finds that states with strong unions generally have a much stronger middle class, while the "10 states with the lowest percentage of workers in unions all have a relatively weak middle class."[46]

Although other factors have also facilitated the growing economic divide in America, careful research suggests that the decline of organized labor is a significant driver. According to research by Martin Asher and Robert Defina in the *Journal of Labor Research,* "decreases in private-sector union density have accounted for about 25 percent of the overall rise in earnings inequality during the past 15 years. Decompositions based on public-sector earnings indicate that increases in union density have produced inequality that is 29 percent below what it otherwise would have been."[47] Likewise, a 2011 study by Bruce Western and Jack Rosenfeld in *American Sociology Review* finds that if union density were today as high as it was in 1973, inequality would be 20 percent lower; and if one accounts for the spillover effect on nonunion wages, inequality

FIGURE 2.2
Union Membership Rate and Middle-Class Share of Aggregate Income, 1969–2009

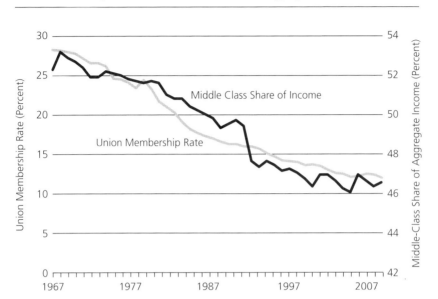

would be one-third lower.[48] Likewise, one study from the 1990s concluded that "40 to 50 percent of the rise in the white-collar premium and 15 to 40 percent of the rise in the college premium are attributable to the fall in union density."[49] Whereas young people once had two open paths to joining the middle-class—get a college education, or join a unionized occupation—over time, the second path has substantially closed.

The Political Impact of Labor's Decline

Apart from the direct effects of organized labor on the economy, the collapse of unions has had a significant impact on the political climate of the United States, weakening the vibrancy of our democracy and blunting legislative efforts to promote economic and social equality. Research suggests that the decline in labor in the 1970s and 1980s is connected to a fall in voter participation.[50] Likewise, the legislative accomplishments of Democratic presidents during the years of labor's dramatic decline—Jimmy Carter, Bill Clinton, and Barack Obama—have been modest compared with the great steps forward under Franklin Roosevelt's New Deal, Harry Truman's Fair Deal, John Kennedy's New Frontier, and Lyndon Johnson's Great Society. Indeed, as Jacob Hacker and Paul Pierson point out, the Carter presidency was marked by fairly conservative economic policies: a cut in the capital gains tax, an increase in the payroll tax, and deregulation.[51] President Clinton is best known for welfare reform and declaring that "the era of big government is over." President Obama's signature initiative on health care, while an important step forward, took a decidedly centrist approach that avoided a single-payer plan and a public option, and was modeled after Republican Governor Mitt Romney's legislation.

In 2004, veteran *Washington Post* columnist David Broder identified the decline of labor over the previous fifty years as one of the biggest changes he had observed in Washington. In the 1950s, "and for decades afterward, the most influential lobbyists did not represent business or trade associations but labor unions," Broder wrote. Labor was "at the forefront of battles for aid to education, civil rights, housing programs and a host of other social causes important to the whole community." The steady weakening of labor since then, Broder wrote, is directly linked to "the decline of progressive politics and with it the near-demise of liberal legislation."[52]

As the role of labor as the "people's lobby" has atrophied, Americans have grown increasingly cynical about government. This change is usually associated with Vietnam and Watergate, but today, there is also a strong belief that politicians put the interests of the wealthy and powerful above those of average Americans. A 2011 *New York Times*/CBS poll found that 69 percent of Americans believe Republicans favor the rich, and a plurality also believes that the Democratic Obama administration favors the wealthy.[53] The evidence suggests that Americans are right to worry about the voice of ordinary Americans in Washington. One study found that, between 1980 and 2003, the government's role in softening economic inequality through taxes on the wealthy and benefit programs for less-advantaged Americans fell by more than one-third.[54]

One can even see the absence of labor's strong voice on the Democratic Party's response to inequality. Missing from the discourse is an emphasis on the value of solidarity and the dignity of all individuals as an important counterbalance to the hyper-competitive and atomized nature of modern markets. Whereas progressives continue to voice the need to push for equal educational opportunity to make our meritocracy more fair (more generous federal aid to elementary and secondary education, and Pell Grants for higher education), there is less sensitivity to the idea that individuals who do not ace the SAT and attend fancy colleges also deserve a solid place in the middle-class by virtue of effort and hard work. Research from David Madland of the Center for American Progress finds that "increasing union membership is as important to rebuilding the middle class as boosting college graduation rates," but one would never know that from the rhetoric of conservative or liberal politicians.[55]

International Comparisons

Some argue that rising economic inequality is an inevitable result of changes in technology and the world economy. The United States has shifted to a knowledge-based economy, which makes skills more important than in the past, and increases returns on education. There is, of course, some truth to this argument, as there is to the contention that globalization puts downward pressure on manufacturing wages in wealthier countries. But a look abroad suggests that other countries continue to have lower levels of inequality than the United States, and that their higher levels of unionization help explain this result.[56]

According to a Bureau of Labor Statistics analysis in *Monthly Law Review* from 2006, many of our major competitors have significantly higher rates of union density. In 2003, 12.4 percent of U.S. wage and salary worker had union membership, compared with a European Union average of 26.3 percent, a rate not seen in the United States since before 1970. Scandinavian countries had rates as high as 78.0 percent (Sweden), 74.1 percent (Finland), 70.4 percent (Denmark), and 53.3 percent (Norway). Ireland and Italy had union densities of 35.3 percent and 33.7 percent, respectively. The United Kingdom had a 29.3 percent density rate, while Canada's union density was 28.4 percent. Australia's unionization rate was 22.9 percent, and Germany, the largest economy in Europe, had a 22.6 percent union density rate. Japan's rate was lower, at 19.7 percent, but still considerably higher than the U.S rate. According to the report, France had a very low union membership rate (8.3 percent), but 95 percent of workers were nevertheless covered by collective bargaining agreements.[57] A 2011 analysis by the Center for Economic and Policy Research, using 2007 data in twenty-one rich countries, likewise finds that union coverage and membership rates are far higher in most other nations. Examining the percentage of workers who are covered by collective bargaining agreements, nine countries (Austria, Belgium, Sweden, Finland, France, Spain, the Netherlands, Denmark, and Italy) had coverage rates of 80 percent or more. Four (Norway, Greece, Portugal, and Germany) had coverage rates between 60 percent and 80 percent. Five (Switzerland, Ireland, Australia, the United Kingdom, and Canada) had coverage rates between 30 percent and 50 percent. And just three—New Zealand, Japan, and the United States—had coverage rates below 20 percent, with the United States at the very bottom of the heap.[58]

Research finds that the countries with higher union density rates and broader collective bargaining coverage also tended to have lower rates of economic inequality, as measured by both wealth and income. In 2000, the United States had one of the highest degrees of wealth inequality in the world. On the Gini index, in which 0 represents perfect equality and 1 represents maximal inequality, the United States had a wealth coefficient of 0.801. Italy, with relatively high union density, had a much lower Gini score (0.609). Likewise, other countries with higher union densities had lower wealth inequality, including the UK (0.697), Canada (0.688), Australia (0.622), Germany (0.677), and Japan (0.547).[59]

An even stronger pattern holds for income inequality. The United States, with very low unionization rates, had the highest Gini coefficient for income of advanced industrial democracies (0.45), according to *The World Factbook,* published by the Central Intelligence Agency. Meanwhile, nations with relatively high union density rates, such as Sweden, Finland, Norway, and Ireland, had much lower Gini scores (0.23 for Sweden, 0.268 for Finland, 0.25 for Norway, and 0.293 for Ireland). Other countries with higher union density rates than the United States also had lower Gini coefficients, including the United Kingdom (0.34), Canada (0.321), Australia (0.305), Germany (0.27), and Japan (0.376).[60] As Figure 2.3 shows, the relationship between low collective bargaining coverage rates and high levels of income inequality is strong.

The Reasons We Should All Care About Rising Inequality

Some argue that we should not care about inequality of economic results; what is far more important is inequality of opportunity.[61] But all Americans, whether or not they care about rising inequality of results per se, should be concerned with the consequences of inequality, for three sets of reasons.

FIGURE 2.3

Income Inequality versus Collective Bargaining Coverage in Twenty-One Countries

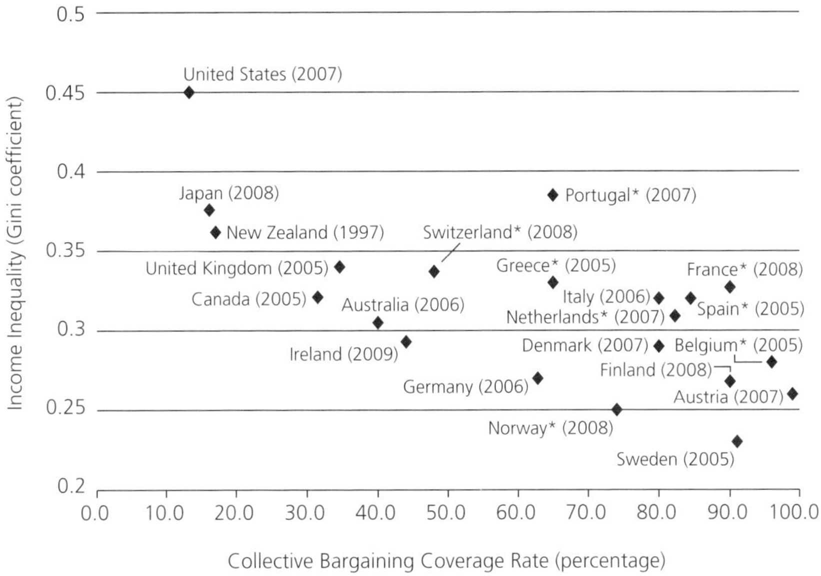

Sources: John Schmitt and Alexandra Mitukiewicz, "Politics Matters: Changes in Unionization Rates in Rich Countries, 1960–2010," Center for Economic and Policy Research, November 2011, figure 2.5. Income inequality data from "Distribution of Family Income: Gini Index," CIA *World Factbook*, https://www.cia.gov/library/publications/the-world-factbook/fields/2172.html.

First, grossly unequal results in one generation necessarily translate into unequal opportunities in the next generation, as wealthy parents pass on considerable advantages to their children and disadvantaged parents pass on disadvantages to their offspring. Nations with large income gaps also tend to have low levels of social mobility, a relationship that economist Alan Kreuger has dubbed "the Great Gatsby Curve."[62] As Americans have seen increases in inequality of results, they have also seen decreases in intergenerational social mobility. The United States now has less intergenerational social mobility than nations such as Australia, Sweden, Spain, France, and Canada.[63] According to the Brookings Institution, Denmark, Norway, and Finland have three times more social mobility than the United States, and Germany has one-and-one-half times more mobility.[64]

Second, starkly unequal economic results weaken our society's commitment to democratic equality, as very wealthy interests increasingly play an outsized role in determining who gets elected to office. Theodore Roosevelt, for example, warned about the growth of "a small class of enormously wealthy and economically powerful men, whose chief object is to hold and increase their power."[65] With inequality at record heights in the United States, Nobel-Prize winning economist Michael Spence told Nicholas Kristof that we have seen "an evolution from one propertied man, one vote; to one man, one vote; to one person, one vote; trending to one dollar, one vote."[66]

Third, dramatically unequal economic results, in which productivity gains increasingly accrue to the very wealthiest members of society, weaken middle-class consumer demand, which drives economic growth in modern economies.[67] In the recent economic downturn, for example, the U.S. economy, with its highly unequal income distribution, continues to struggle, while Germany, which provides among the globe's strongest set of worker protections and has a vibrant middle-class, has one of the world's best performing economies.[68] It is noteworthy that the last time the top 1 percent commanded as much income in the United States as it does today was 1928, just prior to the onset of the Great Depression.[69]

Conclusion

Taken together, the cumulative evidence makes very clear that we should all worry about the growing economic inequality in the United States that is associated with the precipitous decline in the American labor movement. Labor has traditionally provided a strong counterweight to corporate interests, and the collapse of unions in the United States has coincided with skyrocketing economic inequality and a major shift in the country's political climate, making progressive social change harder and harder to accomplish. International comparisons underline these links. All in all, Americans have an enormous amount at stake in the shape of public policies that will help determine whether organized labor will continue to spiral downward or could potentially witness something of a renaissance.

CHAPTER THREE

Why U.S. Labor Has Declined

The Failure of the National Labor Relations Act

What explains the rapid decline in private sector union density out-lined in the previous chapter? Three major possibilities stand out. First, economic globalization and changes in technology may explain some of the drop as increased competition makes it hard for high-wage unionized industries to compete against nonunion low-wage workers abroad. There is some evidence for this contention, though we shall see it is hardly a complete explanation.[1] Second, in theory, decreased member-ship in unions could be a manifestation of worker preference not to join a union, given that modern legislation such as the Occupational Safety and Health Act has reduced the type of abusive behavior by employers that gave rise to unionism in earlier eras. While this idea has some intuitive appeal, survey evidence presented in this chapter suggests the opposite is true: that the proportion of workers wishing to join a union is not declin-ing but rising. Rather, as the data in this chapter show, a third possibility has far greater explanatory power: employer conduct and weak regula-tions have led directly to decreased unionization in America. Indeed, a comparison of different statutory regimes covering different industries leads to the likely conclusion that, under neutral conditions and strong protections, workers overwhelmingly choose to join or form a union. Unfortunately, the National Labor Relations Act (NLRA), which covers most American employees, provides neither strong protections nor pro-motes neutral conditions.

The Incomplete Nature of the Globalization Hypothesis

Some have argued that the decline in unionization in the United States is largely the result of radical shifts in the economy brought about by increased globalization and technology, and "that unions are incompatible with the emerging, increasingly globalized, high tech, service economy."[2] Unions are treated as artifacts of an industrial and manufacturing economy that is waning in America. According to this assumption, which links unionization to manufacturing, declines in manufacturing would necessarily lead to natural declines in unionization. However, this assumption does not take into account that the vast majority of public sector employees that are permitted to unionize have unionized, even though the public sector engages in no manufacturing. The assumption also looks at America in isolation, without any comparison to other countries that are similarly witnessing radical shifts in technology and globalization in order to investigate whether they too are experiencing "natural" declines in unionization.

But as we saw in chapter 2, other nations continue to have much higher rates of union density than the United States. John Schmitt and Alexandra Mitukiewicz's study for the Center for Economic and Policy Research (CEPR) that analyzed twenty-one rich economies over the last half-century demolishes the hypothesis that factors such as shifting economics, technology, globalization, trade, and the like determine union levels. "If the decline in unionization is the inevitable response to the twin forces of globalization and technology," the authors note, "then we would expect unionization rates to follow a similar path in other countries subjected to roughly similar levels of globalization and technology."[3] In fact, they found that neither globalization nor technology "mechanically determines national levels of unionization."[4] The data revealed that politics was the determinative factor in the levels of unionization:

> One simple factor, however, does appear to explain much of the observed variation in unionization trends: the broad national political environment. Countries that have been strongly identified during the postwar period with social democratic parties—Sweden, Denmark, Norway, and Finland—have generally seen small increases in union coverage and only small decreases in union membership since 1980. Over the same period, countries that are more typically identified as "liberal market economies"—the United States, the United Kingdom, Australia, New Zealand, Ireland, Canada,

and Japan—have generally seen sharp drops in union coverage and membership. Countries in the broad Christian democratic tradition, sometimes referred to as "coordinated market economies" or "continental market economies"—Germany, Austria, Italy, the Netherlands, Belgium, France, and Switzerland—typically have had outcomes somewhere in between, with small drops in union coverage and moderate declines in union membership. These patterns are consistent with the view that national politics are a more important determinant of recent trends in unionization than globalization or technological change.[5]

The CEPR study confirms the findings of previous research by University of California–Berkeley's John Logan and others that American unions are not unique with regard to the economic and globalization forces that they face, and that their decline is more a function of the political, legal, social, and business attitudes unique to America.[6] Canadian economist W. Craig Riddell, for example, notes that in 1960, the United States and Canada both had roughly 30 percent of wage and salary workers in unions, but by 2000, while union density in Canada remained about 30 percent, in the United States the share had dropped by half. Riddell found that the difference primarily was explained not by structural differences in the economy, but rather by differences in the laws governing union organizing in the two countries.[7]

The Weakness of the Hypothesis Suggesting Workers No Longer Want to Join Unions

Likewise, while some suggest declining unionization represents worker dissatisfaction with unions, data show an overall increase in workers' desire to join or form a union. Based on available data between 1947 and 2005, the number of Americans that approve of unions has always exceeded the number that disapproves.[8] Union population has declined some since 2009, but careful analysis suggests this largely reflects public anger about the economy and support for unions is likely to grow again as the economy recovers.[9] Not only do Americans generally approve of unions, but a majority of them also want the unions to have either increased or sustaining levels of influence over "social outcomes," with 38 percent responding that they wanted unions to have increased influence and 29 percent responding that union influence should remain constant.[10] A 2011 Gallup poll, likewise, found that Americans are three times as likely to identify big business as the biggest threat to the country rather than big labor.[11]

Polling data has also shown that, between 1984 and 2004, there has been a consistent increase in the desire among nonunion employees to join a union.[12] Hart Research Associates found that approximately one-third of all nonunion workers in the 1980s wanted union representation, approximately 40 percent of all nonunion workers in the 1990s wanted union representation, and starting in 2002, a majority of nonunion workers wanted union representation. Based on these figures, the noted Harvard labor economist Richard Freeman has concluded that, in the mid-1990s, "analysis suggested that if all the workers who wanted union representation could achieve it, then 44% of the workforce would have union representation."[13] This degree of union density would be almost four times current levels, indicating that decreased levels of unionization in no way reflects worker preferences.

Unions' Decline Has Been Caused, in Large Part, by a Lack of Legal Protections for Union Organizers

While the globalization and worker attitude hypotheses are incomplete or weak, there is much stronger evidence to suggest that unbalanced American labor laws and corporatist culture explain the decline in union-ization. The struggle to join or form a union is no easy task. In addition to the usual efforts involved in organizing any group of individuals for a common cause, organizing a union has the added difficulty of requir-ing individuals to place their jobs on the line for something that may not ultimately come to fruition.

Though the NLRA was structured to create a space where employees would not have to risk losing their jobs to exercise their rights, it has not fulfilled its mission. While the law strictly forbids taking action against employees trying to organize, both employers and employees know that the law offers little protection.

Aggressive Lawbreaking by Employers

In labor's heyday, employers mostly followed the law. But over time, as union strength and political support waned, employers became increas-ingly aggressive in their stance toward organization. Harvard Law

Professor Paul Weiler's groundbreaking 1983 study found that, between 1957 and 1980, the number of employees entitled to reinstatement increased 1,000 percent due to employer unfair labor practices.[14] Weiler found that one in twenty union supporters were fired during election campaigns, while the AFL-CIO puts the figure at closer to one in eight.[15] These sorts of terminations send a message to other union supporters that they risk their jobs if they exercise their legal right to organize a union.

More recently, between 1999 and 2003, employers illegally discharged employees in over a third of all union organizing drives conducted under National Labor Relations Board (NLRB) supervision.[16] In addition to discharges, employers also altered benefits or working conditions in 22 percent of organizing drives, and engaged in harassment and discipline of union activists in 41 percent of organizing drives.[17] When employers engage in this sort of conduct, there is no ambiguity in the message. The employer conveys that union supporters "put their jobs on the line" by exercising their rights—this is the message that employers want to send.

The increase in the incidents of unfair labor practices on the part of employers has caused a steady increase in the number of cases brought before the NLRB. Between 1955 and 1978, the number of complaints brought before the NLRB increased from approximately 6,000 to 40,000.[18] Though the number has dropped to its current level of 16,000 complaints in 2009, this is largely due to the combined factors of decreasing union density in the past two decades, and the unions' strategic decision to bypass the NLRB because it is ineffective.[19] Of these 16,000 complaints, more than one-third were regarding discrimination and termination targeted at pro-union employees.[20] As high as this figure seems, it represents only a portion of the actual number of unfair labor practices, especially with regards to those surrounding organizing campaigns. In Kate Bronfenbrenner's report for the Economic Policy Institute, she estimates that less than half of all unfair labor practices are reported.[21] She notes there are extreme disincentives in almost every situation of reporting an unfair labor practice. In instances where the union believes that there is a high probability of winning an election, unions often make a strategic decision to put up with the employer's illegal activity for fear that reporting it will allow the employer to indefinitely delay or block the election.[22] In instances where the union has lost an election due to unfair labor practices, it is difficult—and often impossible—to convince employees to come forward and testify on behalf of improperly fired coworkers because many fear employer reprisals.[23] In addition to the disincentives of reporting illegal employer activity, there is little positive incentive to come forward—even if one is ultimately successful in the charge—because awards are generally paltry.[24]

Public versus Private Sector Organizing

A comparison between those employees covered under the NLRA and those covered under public sector labor laws is revealing. Though many of the public sector labor laws are modeled after the NLRA, public sector employers—local, state, and federal governments—create a neutral environment under which unions may organize at a much higher rate than in the private sector. This is true for a variety of reasons, from the governments' generally reduced ideological opposition to labor to its greater public accountability for any anti-union activities. The result is an environment where nearly half of all organizing campaigns in the public sector have met no opposing campaign by the employer.[25] While in the other half of public sector campaigns, when the employer engaged in some of the same tactics found in the private sector, they rarely reach the scale of the private sector. According to Bronfenbrenner:

> Three percent discharged workers for union activity or made unilateral changes in wages and benefits, 22% held captive audience meetings, and 2% held supervisory one-on-ones at least weekly. Not surprisingly, both win rates and first contract rates continue to remain much higher in the public sector, averaging 84% overall. But in the few cases where unions are faced with moderate or aggressive employer opposition, the win rate plummets, suggesting that they are ill-prepared for the kind of opposition that has become routine under the NLRB.[26]

The significantly lower rate of anti-union tactics has allowed public sector unionization to increase significantly. This is true despite the fact that such unionization is not permitted in many states, meaning that where it is allowed, union density is quite high.

Indeed, public sector organizing, which is governed by individual state laws, provides in some ways the mirror-opposite picture of private sector organizing since the mid-twentieth century. Very few public sector workers (teachers, fire fighters, police, social workers, and so on) were organized until states began authorizing public sector collective bargaining, beginning with Wisconsin in the late 1950s.[27]

In the 1960s, organizing of teachers and other public employees increased dramatically, so that by 1974, roughly one in four public workers was in a union, the same proportion of workers organized in the private sector.[28] But while private sector union density subsequently fell to 6.9 percent in 2010, public sector union density rose to 36.2 percent.[29] So dramatic has been the increase in public sector organizing and the decrease in private sector organizing that in 2010 the Bureau of Labor Statistics reported that for the first time in history, there were more public sector union members in the United States than private sector members, even though public sector workers make up a much smaller proportion of the overall workforce.[30] As Barry T. Hirsch of Georgia State University notes:

> At the same time that private sector unionism was in decline, public sector unionism increased rapidly in the 1960s and 1970s following enactment of enabling public sector labor laws within (most) states and for federal employees. . . . Although the size of the public sector has grown considerably since the 1970s, density has remained relatively constant, rising from 32.8 percent in 1977 to 36.7 percent in 1983 to a current level of 36.2 percent in 2010.[31]

The primary difference between private and public sector unions comes down to the levels at which the employer opposes the union, often unlawfully.[32] As Thomas Geoghegan notes, because the NLRA does not apply, "the public sector is the only place where unions can organize without being maimed. It is like crossing into Canada," where laws are more union friendly.[33]

Private Sector Anti-Union Consultants

The increase in private sector employer opposition can be seen in the decrease of consent elections and increase in employers' use of anti-labor consultants. These indicators are useful because presence of the former usually represents situations where the employer has mounted little or no anti-union campaign, while presence of the latter usually represents situations where the employer will engage in all legal (and sometimes illegal) activity to defeat the union. A consent election is one where the union and employer have been able to come to agreement with regard to the details of the election and the description of the appropriate bargaining unit, thereby allowing an informal election. Consent elections used to be common when many employers accepted that employees had a right to join a union, and that if the employees voted for a union, there was little that could be done. In 1960, 42.2 percent of certification elections resulted from employer consent agreements. By 1978, that number had dropped to 7.9 percent.[34] Between 1999 and 2004, only 1.13 percent of elections were governed by consent agreements rather than a NLRB hearing.[35]

Increasingly, the pre-election issues have become part of the battleground to decrease the likelihood that the unions will succeed in organizing. Professor John Lawler of the University of Illinois has found that all other factors being equal, under consent elections, unions obtain 8 percent to 10 percent more of the vote and have a 10 percent higher victory rate.[36] Professor William Cooke, director of the Michigan State University School of Human Resources and Labor Relations, has advanced two reasons why workers are more likely to vote for the union in consent elections:

> First, by consenting to an election, employers signal workers that they do not strongly oppose collective bargaining, or even if they do, they believe that there is little reason to fight it in this particular case. One can imagine, for example, that many employers already largely unionized do not find it profitable to oppose the inclusion of one more work unit under their contract. This signal to workers will increase their estimate of the utility of unionization, since the employer presumably does not campaign actively to convince them otherwise. Second, since the unit requested by the union is not modified in a consent election, the unit does not take on new group dynamics by the addition or subtraction of job classifications or plants. In stipulated elections, on the other hand, it is presumed that employers campaign more actively against unionization, and the unit originally requested is frequently modified.[37]

These explanations show how fragile a budding organizing drive is, even if the employees support the union, meaning that subtle changes in the composition of the group or the employer's messaging can have significant impacts on the results.

Anti-union consultants were a minor factor several decades ago, but have now become a $4 billion-a-year industry, often narrowly skirting or overtly violating the law.[38] As of 2004, 76 percent of employers hired union-busting consultants prior to a certification election.[39] The consultants represent the polar opposite of the consent elections, as the employer has decided to spend significant sums of money to bring in sophisticated outside personnel to ensure that the employees do not organize a union. John Logan writes:

> Consultants not only advise employers on how to conduct an anti-union campaign, but also develop, implement and monitor the campaign. They usually work behind the scenes, and train supervisors on how to interrogate, intimidate and terrify employees. They are effectively running the workplace for the duration of the campaign. Consultants use a variety of methods to convey their aggressive anti-union message—impersonal communication mechanisms, such as anti-union newsletters, and videos, interpersonal mechanisms, such as group "captive audience" meetings (which, in any other walk of life, would be considered a form of unlawful imprisonment), and personal mechanisms, especially one-on-one meetings between supervisors and employees. While consultant campaigns have become significantly more sophisticated in recent years, their fundamental tactics have remained remarkably stable since the 1970s. The most significant innovations in recent years include the greater use of information technology (anti-union videos, DVDs and websites) and the greater diversity of consultant personnel.[40]

The use of anti-union consultants has proliferated because they are effective. Their techniques—whether legal or not—hinder organizing, and effectively convey to employees the employer's strong disapproval of the union, and the lengths to which the employer may go in expressing that disapproval.

Why the NLRB Fails to Protect Unionizing Employees

Unionizing drives are intense, real-time affairs, where access to employees is limited, power structures are uneven, and misinformation and fear are constant problems. An effective legal structure for labor would provide either quick injunctive remedies or large damage awards to aggrieved employees in order to provide them a modicum of legal power to balance against the overwhelming economic power of the employer. Ideally, the law would provide both in order to give the employees a level of security under which they could express their preferences with regard to unionization. The NLRB provides neither.

Lengthy Delays

The NLRB process was designed to move quickly, which is why there is virtually no discovery or other pretrial matters that often slow down litigation. In spite of these devices to speed up the process, it still often takes years to make it through the NLRB process, which is ultimately not self-enforcing.[41] In 2009, in instances where the NLRB reached a decision following the issuance of an Unfair Labor Practice (ULP) complaint, it took a median of 483 days for the decision to be reached.[42] For cases pending before the NLRB as of September 30, 2009, the median time since the filing of a ULP charge was 963 days.[43]

Inadequate Remedies

Beyond the lack of speed to decision, the NLRB remedies are also woefully inadequate to provide relief for aggrieved employees or to hinder employer misconduct. In 2009, 14,825 employees were awarded a total of $76,337,306 in back-pay resulting from an unfair labor practice complaint to the NLRB—an average of $5,149 per employee.[44] Under the current law, an employee who is fired for attempting to organize a union has a duty to search for alternate employment, and if successful at the NLRB, any money the employee made at her new job will be deducted from the award.[45] Therefore, in a situation where a janitor making minimum wage is fired for trying to organize, and she turns around and finds another job as a janitor making minimum wage, she may go through three years of NLRB process, succeed, and receive no monetary damages.[46] Instead, she will be offered her old job at her old pay, and the employer will have to post notice that it will not engage in such behavior again. Furthermore, since 80 percent of employees who win reinstatement will be fired again within a year, even this award is often illusory.[47] Thomas Geoghegan makes the point vividly: "So if you put on a union button, it's not just that you'll be fired. You're fired and never coming back, ever: and if you try it, you'll be fired again within a year."[48] During the interim, other employees will have heard the message clearly: the law will not protect you or reward you; if you organize you will be fired.

Even if the employer acts egregiously, willfully, and openly flouts the law, the NLRB has no authority to impose punitive penalties.[49] And an aggrieved employee may not simply circumvent the NLRB, as its jurisdiction under the NLRA is exclusive, preempting state laws in the field.[50] This point cannot be overemphasized. The harassment, discrimination, or termination of employees for union activity normally would implicate a host of other state tort issues that in other circumstances may provide the employee some protection or relief. However, the courts have been clear that the NLRA preempts these state laws, and its weak procedures and remedies are the only avenue available for most aggrieved employees.

Viewed from the employer's perspective, it is no surprise that open disregard of the NLRA has become the norm. Though the unions and employer have a strong shared interest in the success of the enterprise, their interests diverge sharply with regard to the distribution of earnings. Simply stated, employers seek to maximize their profits by minimizing all costs as much as possible, including labor costs, while unions seek to distribute as much of the corporation's revenues as possible to the workers.[51] Furthermore, unions want to create a space wherein the employees can exercise real power and have a real voice in the management of the corporation, while employers often see this concession as a dangerous affront to efficient management. Whether it is simply a rhetorical tool or the employers truly believe it, they often frame the forming of a union as the site of conflict that will drain the common resources of the corporation. In a confidential memorandum sent from the offices of Littler Mendelson—a notorious "union-busting" firm—companies were advised to frame the anti-union argument in these very terms:

> Tell the employees that if they select a paid agent to represent them (the union), the Company will probably have to hire lawyers or other experts to represent the Company. This will be an expense to both of you, and you would rather iron out problems with the employees directly, while both of you keep your money. . . . Point out the indirect costs of unionization that you want to avoid: executive time spent in bargaining sessions, working time of employees sent on union business, cost of hiring lawyers and other labor relations experts. Money spent for such costs obviously cannot go to the employees in higher wages.[52]

Beyond these high-level ideological differences, employers view unionization as a significant cost for good reason. As outlined in chapter 2, union members invariably have higher salaries and better benefits than their nonunion counterparts. According to the Bureau of Labor Statics, in 2010, among full-time wage and salary workers, union members made 28 percent more than nonunion members.[53] Substantial union premiums held true within occupations, including service sector employees, sales/

office occupations, and transportation workers.[54] In addition to higher wages, as noted earlier, a higher percentage of unionized employees have health and pension benefits, and in cases where both groups of employees have benefits, the benefits tend to be superior for unionized employees.[55] Professor John W. Budd of the University of Minnesota observes:

> In sum, the broad pattern of results reported by Freeman (1981) and Freeman and Medoff (1984) remains true 30 years later. Jobs that are represented by a union have total expenditures on voluntary benefit items significantly higher than similar nonunion jobs— between 15 and 40 percent higher with total compensation held constant, and perhaps as much as 70 percent higher overall.[56]

Faced with increased salary and benefit costs, concession in sole control over the running of the enterprise, and an extremely weak statutory scheme, it is not at all surprising that many employers simply disregard the NLRA.[57] As Thomas Geoghegan has starkly noted:

> Breaking the law, i.e., firing people, is absurdly cheap. . . . The best deal in America, in cold business terms. There is a famous study, somewhere, that says a union on average will increase a company's wage bill by 20 percent. . . . And the penalty for violating the Wagner act is what . . . what, $3,000 a crack? Paid one time only, three or four years from now? An employer who didn't break the law would have to be what economists call an "irrational firm."[58]

Geoghegan's example provides wonderful fodder for legal ethics classes. Does an employer-side attorney have an ethical duty to disclose studies that reveal that firing the organizers—while illegal—would save the company much more than the company would ever have to pay if found liable for the firings? It is hard to imagine any other area of law where a lawyer conceivably may be subject to malpractice for *not* counseling her client to break the law.

Comparison to the Railway Labor Act

In understanding how the various provisions of the NLRA affect the reality on the ground, it is helpful to look at another major statute that covers one group of private sector employees explicitly excluded under the NLRA: rail and airline workers. The Railway Labor Act (RLA) preceded the NLRA by about a decade in 1926, and was passed in order to bring stability to the rail industry. Therefore, when the NLRA was passed in 1935, it explicitly excluded in its definitions of "employee" and "employer" all parties covered under the RLA. Currently, railway and airline employees comprise the two main groups covered under the RLA.

The RLA has certain requirements that make it much more difficult to organize a union. Prime among these is the requirement, as one union group notes, "that a majority of a company's employees at ALL company locations must vote for the union—not just those at any one location. This requires workers to reach out across huge geographical areas, as many of them are covered by national companies."[59] This is in contrast to the rules of the NLRA under which the employer and union can either agree to the size and definition of the appropriate bargaining unit, or the NLRB determines the unit based on individual circumstances. Moreover, until a rule change in 2010, elections under the RLA followed a strange rule used in few other election situations—that the union needed to receive support from a majority of all eligible employees, not just of votes cast, meaning nonvoters were effectively counted as a vote against the union.[60] These differences help explain why, in 1996, FedEx employees sought to be governed by the NLRA, while FedEx management sought to stay categorized as an airline governed under the RLA. Having to reach 80,000 far-flung FedEx employees posed a daunting obstacle to union organizers.[61]

In spite of these significant burdens to unionization, Southern Methodist University professor Charles Morris notes that workers under the RLA still have a very high level of union density. As of the mid-1990s, Morris reports that, of a total of 257,000 employees of the Class I, II, and III rail carriers, between 80 and 85 percent were represented by unions; and for the scheduled airlines of the 591,300 nonmanagerial employees, some 65 to 70 percent were represented by unions. These numbers represented increases in union density over the 1980s.[62]

There are a variety of reasons for this extraordinary fact. As Morris points out, one reason may be historical. Another reason is that, although certain provisions of the RLA may make it more difficult to organize, the National Mediation Board—the federal agency responsible for conducting the representation process and assisting the parties with collective bargaining and arbitration—has been more willing than the NLRB to "step . . . into the fray to ease such burdens."[63] Most significantly, if an employee is fired for trying to organize a union, she can seek immediate injunctive relief in federal court, and be reinstated quickly, thereby neutralizing the chilling effect of firing union organizers. Morris has found that the availability of this mechanism has such a strong deterrent effect that discriminatory discharges are virtually nonexistent for employees covered under the RLA: "no carrier wants to risk [a union taking the credit for an employee being re-hired] just prior to an NMB representation election."[64]

Conclusion

The significantly greater union densities found under the RLA and public sector laws illustrate that there is a strong correlation between the NLRA's inability to protect workers in exercising their right to organize and the shrinking labor movement in America. Explanations for this phenomenon that are based on increased worker disinterest cannot explain why workers similar in every respect, except the laws that govern their labor relations, act so differently when it comes to organizing. In statutory schemes that provide employees a greater degree of freedom from government and employer interference in whether to organize, workers choose to organize at much higher rates. Similarly, the hypothesis that union decline is the result of increased globalization and changes in technology cannot adequately account for why countries that are experiencing similar levels of globalization are witnessing different effects on their workforce with regard to organization. Political, legal, and sociocultural factors play a major role in producing healthy levels of union density.

CHAPTER FOUR

The United States as an International Outlier in Protecting Labor Rights

How does the U.S. protection of labor rights compare with that of other countries? Rhetorically, the United States has been at the vanguard in promoting the fundamental right to labor organization, having participated in and pushed early on for international recognition and articulations of these basic rights. However, in practice and effect, the United States has fallen behind in promoting unionization as national policy and creating environments in which workers are protected in organizing.

The United States is nearly alone among industrialized democracies in not treating the ability to organize as a core democratic value and a human right. The nation's aberrant position with regard to unionization as a human right is especially strange, because America was largely responsible for the conception and adoption of this universal norm. This is not just a case where America should adopt international policies because they are more in line with our own democratic values. This is an instance where America should adopt the very policies that it originally promoted in the name of human dignity and peace.

This chapter will outline the landscape of international law concerning labor, a landscape that the United States had an important hand in creating. It will show that there is an international consensus that the ability to organize and be a member of a union free from external intimidation is a fundamental human right. Though America was integral to forming this consensus, it currently stands alone among industrialized democracies in not signing international protocols that support the rights to organize. We will then perform a brief comparison of American labor law and the domestic laws of several other western democracies to show that American rules are also far weaker than those of its European counterparts. Not only has the United States refused to join international conventions that commit it to protecting workers' rights, its domestic laws are among the weakest, while U.S. business opposition to unions is among the fiercest. This combination leaves American workers exposed, vulnerable, and often unable to make the free choice of whether or not to join a union.

Union Membership Is Internationally Recognized as a Human Right

In 1944, the United States convened a meeting of the four major world powers at the Dumbarton Oaks mansion in Washington, D.C. At the time, the energies of the developed nations had been consumed for the better part of the century by preparing for, waging, or recovering from two world wars. Because it had become clear that individual states could no longer be trusted to protect their own people through national policies, there was a need to create international institutions that would define and promote universal values and protect basic human rights. The purpose of the meeting at Dumbarton Oaks was for the great powers to articulate and adopt a position on these universal rights and to create the framework for an international organization suited to promote these values.[1] As German professor Christian Tomuschat argues:

> After the horrors of World War II, a broad consensus emerged at the worldwide level demanding that the individual human being be placed under the protection of the international community. . . . Since the lesson learned was that protective mechanisms at the domestic level alone did not provide sufficiently stable safeguards, it became almost self-evident to entrust the planned new world organization with assuming the role of guarantor of human rights on a universal scale.[2]

The United States saw labor unions as a bulwark against both fascism and Communism. By helping smooth the jagged edges of capitalism and building a strong middle-class, organized labor would make Communism less attractive and democracy more likely. And as independent civic institutions, labor unions would provide a check against totalitarian regimes on both the left and the right. Historically, dictators from Hitler to Stalin made sure to destroy organized labor. As American labor leader Albert Shanker explained, "The first thing a dictator does is get rid of the trade unions."[3]

The U.S.-led effort resulted in the Universal Declaration of Human Rights, which was based on the "recognition of the inherent dignity and of the equal and inalienable rights of all members of the human family [as] the foundation of freedom, justice and peace in the world."[4] Even though the declaration is not legally binding, the United States played a central role in the drafting it and joined in the unanimous vote to adopt it.[5] Article 23 of the Universal Declaration states:

1. Everyone has the right to work, to free choice of employment, to just and favourable conditions of work and to protection against unemployment.
2. Everyone, without any discrimination, has the right to equal pay for equal work.
3. Everyone who works has the right to just and favourable remuneration ensuring for himself and his family an existence worthy of human dignity, and supplemented, if necessary, by other means of social protection.
4. Everyone has the right to form and to join trade unions for the protection of his interests.

Similarly, Article 22 of the American Declaration of the Rights and Duties of Man, adopted by the Organization of American States several months prior to the Universal Declaration, states that, "Every person has the right to associate with others to promote, exercise and protect his legitimate interests of a political, economic, religious, social, cultural, professional, labor union or other nature."[6] These documents—both of which had the United States as a central actor in creating and promoting them—provide clear articulation of the ability to form a labor organization as a fundamental human right that must be protected by all nations.

These articulations of the international consensus that the opportunity to organize is a human right were not limited to the postwar years, when exhaustion with conflict pushed states to make broad rules for peace. Following passage of the Universal Declaration and the American Declaration in the late 1940s, the United Nations set out to articulate the broad principles of human rights. The United Nations understood that one could not separate out and protect civil and political rights without also similarly protecting social and cultural rights.[7] Recent wars had shown that the assaults on human rights did not make that fine distinction, and neither could the protections. The U.N. Commission on Human Rights completed its work on articulating a set of universal human rights in 1954, and after much debate the United Nations passed two parallel covenants, one for political and civil rights and the other for social, economic, and cultural rights. Article 8 of The International Covenant on Economic, Social and Cultural Rights of 1966 focuses on the central role that unions play in ensuring democratic values and human rights, requiring states to ensure:

a. The right of everyone to form trade unions and join the trade union of his choice, subject only to the rules of the organization concerned, for the promotion and protection of his economic and social interests. No restrictions may be placed on the exercise of this right other than those prescribed by law and which are necessary in a democratic society in the interests of national security or public order or for the protection of the rights and freedoms of others;

b. The right of trade unions to establish national federations or confederations and the right of the latter to form or join international trade-union organizations;

c. The right of trade unions to function freely subject to no limitations other than those prescribed by law and which are necessary in a democratic society in the interests of national security or public order or for the protection of the rights and freedoms of others;[8]

Similarly, the International Covenant on Civil and Political Rights (ICCPR) of 1966 recognized that labor rights were implicated not only in the economic sphere, but in the civil and political spheres as well. The ICCPR is the primary instrument used to enforce rights by the United Nations Human Rights Committee. The ICCPR requires states to submit reports at regular intervals on topics under the purview of the Human Rights Committee. The committee assesses each state and its compliance with international norms of human rights. Though these assessments are not legally binding, "states are expected to live up in good faith to the views addressed to them by the Committee."[9] The ICCPR limits state and private actors from hindering the rights to organize or join a union. Specifically, Article 22 of the ICCPR states:

1. Everyone shall have the right to freedom of association with others, including the right to form and join trade unions for the protection of his interests.
2. No restrictions may be placed on the exercise of this right other than those which are prescribed by law and which are necessary in a democratic society in the interests of national security or public safety, public order (ordre public), the protection of public health or morals or the protection of the rights and freedoms of others. This article shall not prevent the imposition of lawful restrictions on members of the armed forces and of the police in their exercise of this right.
3. Nothing in this article shall authorize States Parties to the International Labour Organisation Convention of 1948 concerning Freedom of Association and Protection of the Right to Organize to take legislative measures which would prejudice, or to apply the law in such a manner as to prejudice, the guarantees provided for in that Convention.[10]

Three years after the ICCPR was established, in 1969, the American Convention on Human Rights—signed by nations in South, Central, and North America—reaffirmed the right to join a labor organization as a central component of the freedom of association. Article 16 of the convention states, "Everyone has the right to associate freely for ideological, religious, political, economic, labor, social, cultural, sports, or other purposes."[11] The convention created the Inter-American Court of Human Rights, which provides a forum and procedures for dealing with violations by signatories and non-signatories.[12] The United States has not ratified this convention, in large part because of opposition to clauses that could be interpreted to prohibit abortion and the death penalty, rather than the convention's position on labor rights.[13]

In addition to conventions promulgated by international political organizations, the nongovernmental Organisation for Economic Cooperation and Development's (OECD) guidelines for multinational enterprises promulgated in 1976 emphasizes a respect for union rights. It counsels multinationals to "respect the right of their employees to be represented by trade unions and other bona fide representatives of employees, and engage in constructive negotiations, either individually or through employers' associations, with such representatives with a view to reaching agreements on employment conditions."[14]

The International Labour Organization

The International Labour Organization (ILO) provides perhaps the strongest guarantees of organizational rights of any established and well-respected international body. The ILO is one of the oldest multinational organizations still in existence, founded in 1919 as a part of the League of Nations and later absorbed by the United Nations. Its primary purpose is to help shape international standards for labor and labor organizing and to report information pertaining to labor practices around the world. It was awarded the Nobel Peace Price in 1969 for its work.[15] The composition of the ILO takes into account the varying interests that exist with regard to unionization. Therefore, every nation is afforded three representatives—one from the government, one representing labor interests, and one representing employers' interests. In this unusual composition, the ILO is one of the only international organizations that accepts delegations that do not represent governments.[16] The freedom of association is the motivating principle behind the ILO:

> The principle of freedom of association is set out in the Preamble to the Constitution, as adopted in 1919. This text identifies this principle as one of the essential means of preserving lasting peace in the world. It was forcibly re-emphasized in the Declaration of Philadelphia concerning the aims and purposes of the International Labour Organization, adopted on 10 May 1944 and annexed to the Constitution in 1946, which identifies freedom of association as being essential to sustained progress. . . .
>
> Under the terms of these constitutional texts, while freedom of association is essential for lasting universal peace and sustained progress, it is also a fundamental requirement for the ILO itself in view of its tripartite nature. By guaranteeing the representation of workers and employers, alongside governments, the principle of freedom of association constitutes a guarantee for the good functioning of the ILO.[17]

The ILO's emphasis on freedom of association stems from the belief that social and economic justice is essential for maintaining peaceful societies. These cannot be achieved without individuals having the right to free speech, association, and organization.

The ILO has eight "Core Conventions" and a variety of other conventions related to workers' rights. Using the principles outlined in the

Convention on Freedom of Association and Protection of the Right to Organize ("C87") and the Convention on the Right to Organize and Collective Bargaining ("C98"), the ILO created the Committee on Freedom of Association. The purpose of this agency is to find facts, resolve disputes, and generally protect the freedom of workers to associate with one another by forming labor unions.[18]

The United States' involvement with the ILO has been complicated, not simply splitting along well-worn party lines. The United States joined the ILO in 1936, and remained a member continuously for over forty years. However, under President Jimmy Carter the United States temporarily withdrew from the organization from1977 to 1980 to protest the ILO's recognition of state-controlled unions in the Soviet Bloc as legitimate representatives of workers.[19] Similarly, even conservative presidents skeptical of domestic labor unions have recognized the potential for the ILO in reaffirming human rights and fighting tyrannical regimes. President Ronald Reagan used the ILO to empower workers and unions in the Soviet Union and South Africa and thereby undermine state control. Kimberly Elliott of the Center for Global Development and Harvard labor economist Richard Freeman note, "In 1982, with strong backing from the United States, ILO conference delegates voted to initiate an Article 26 complaint against Poland for its treatment of the Solidarity trade union. That and strong support for black unions fighting apartheid in South Africa revived the ILO's credibility in the 1980s."[20] Since 1948, when the ILO passed the Freedom of Association and Protection of the Right to Organize Convention, the ability to join or organize a union has been regarded as a basic human right that belongs to each individual. This right extends to all "workers and employers, without distinction whatsoever," and only allows states to exempt police and military from the right to organize.[21] Though the vast majority of nations have ratified this Convention—150 in total—the United States astoundingly is not among them.[22]

While the rights protected by some of the ILO conventions are quite similar to American law, business groups opposed ratifying these conventions because the ILO provides the worker a greater range of protections against violation. This can be seen in the ILO Right to Organize and Collective Bargaining Convention of 1949—which 160 nations have ratified, the United States not among them.[23] Article 1 provides that:

> Workers shall enjoy adequate protection against acts of anti-union discrimination in respect of their employment, both at the

time of entering employment and during the employment relationship. Such protection shall apply more particularly in respect of acts calculated to: make the employment of a worker subject to the condition that he shall not join a union or shall relinquish trade union membership; cause the dismissal of or otherwise prejudice a worker by reason of union membership or because of participation in union activities outside working hours or, with the consent of the employer, within working hours.[24]

Unlike the NLRA, which guarantees the right to organize, but undermines the guarantee with weak penalties, the ILO conventions articulate an additional right to be adequately protected against infringements of their organizing rights. Similarly, Article 2 of the C98 convention focuses on the protective aspects of the right by defining "interference" broadly:

Workers' and employers' organisations shall be protected against interference by each other or each other's agents or members. In particular, acts which are designed to promote the establishment of workers' organizations under the domination of employers or employers' organizations, or to support workers' organizations by financial or other means, with the object of placing such organizations under the control of employers or employers' organisations, shall be deemed to constitute acts of interference.[25]

While the NLRA already prohibits the discharge of employees for union activities, Cornell economists Nancy Chau and S.M. Ravi Kanbur note, "[a]doption of Convention 98 would shift the burden of proof in favor of employees in National Labor Relations Board hearings."[26]

The United States is a member of the ILO, but it has failed to ratify most of the ILO's Core Conventions, making the United States an international outlier. The ILO's eight Core Conventions and number of countries that have ratified them are as follows:

- C29- Forced Labour, 1930 (153 ratifications)
- C87- Freedom of Association and Protection of the Right to Organize, 1948 (131 ratifications)
- C98- Right to Organize and Collective Bargaining, 1949 (147 ratifications)
- C100- Equal remuneration, 1951 (148 ratifications)
- C105- Abolition of Forced Labour, 1957 (146 ratifications)

- C111- Discrimination (Employment and Occupation), 1958(144 ratifications)
- C138- Minimum Age Convention, 1973 (99 ratifications)
- C182- Elimination of the Worst Forms of Child Labour, 1999 (37 ratifications)[27]

A brief review of even the titles of these Conventions shows that they are in line with fundamental American values. Of these eight Core Conventions, the United States has ratified only two: C105 (Abolition of Forced Labour) and C182 (Elimination of the Worst Forms of Child Labour), sending the message that America is not willing to commit to the idea that the remaining topics involve universal individual human rights.[28]

A recent ILO case illustrates the importance of these international human rights standards, while also showing America's occasional failure to live up to basic requirements. In 2005, the United Electrical, Radio and Machine Workers of America (UE) brought a case before the ILO challenging a North Carolina statute that prohibits public employees from bargaining collectively by declaring any agreement or contract between a labor organization and any governmental body to be illegal and null and void.[29] In addition to workers being denied their basic rights of association, UE further alleged that the statute led to "the unmistakable prevalence of widespread race and sex discrimination."[30] UE argued that the United States government was in violation of its obligations under the ILO to protect fundamental labor rights. The United States government responded that the North Carolina workers were not being deprived of fundamental labor rights and that the U.S. government was in full compliance with its ILO obligations.

The ILO adopted the recommendations of its Committee on Freedom of Association (CFA), the governing body tasked with investigating and adjudicating complaints, holding that the U.S. government should "take steps aimed at bringing the state legislation, in particular, through the repeal of NCGS §95-98, into conformity with freedom of association principles, thus ensuring effective recognition of the right of collective bargaining throughout the country's territory."[31] Rather than follow the ILO opinion, however, the U.S. Department of Justice, under President George W. Bush, sent a letter to the special deputy attorney general in North Carolina indicating that it would not be taking any of the ILO recommended actions, stating "The United States government believes that it is in full compliance with any obligations it may have by virtue of its ILO membership."[32] This case shows how the United States's decision not to sign all ILO core conventions concerning labor and worker rights have real effects for workers who face discrimination in America.

United States Labor Law Lags Significantly Behind That of Other Industrialized Nations

American labor law is not only an outlier when compared with international law, but also when compared to the domestic laws of other industrialized democracies. Freedom House, the international research and advocacy group devoted to assessing and promoting democracy worldwide, provides 165 countries a ranking from 0 to 4 based on a worker's rights in each country. According to this ranking, approximately 8 percent of countries receive a score of 0, which indicates "Very Repressive" conditions; 16 percent of countries receive a score of 1, which indicates "Repressive" conditions; approximately 28 percent receive a score of 2, which indicates "Partly Free" conditions; approximately 23 percent receive a score of 3, which indicates "Mostly Free" conditions; and approximately 25 percent receive a score of 4, which indicates "Free" conditions.[33] Freedom House has ranked the United States below at least forty-one other countries, giving it a 3 ("Mostly Free") out of a possible 4 with regard to labor's freedom to organize.[34] The only other fully industrialized nation to receive a lower ranking is Russia,[35] with Japan receiving a ranking equal to America.[36] The report describes America as "the most glaring example" of a country that "otherwise observe[s] a wide array of democratic freedoms . . . [and] may still take steps to limit the power of trade unions as agents of collective bargaining and sources of independent political power."[37] Freedom House reports:

> In recent years, unions have been confronted with mounting resistance by employers. Management has used a variety of tactics to forestall unionization, and has shown a willingness to violate labor law if it would result in the defeat of a union campaign to gain bargaining recognition. When found guilty of violations by the courts or the National Labor Relations Board (NLRB), companies are often given slap-on-the-wrist penalties that fail to discourage management from summarily firing union supporters.[38]

In Western Europe only one country—Turkey—ranks alongside America as "Mostly Free" rather than "Free."[39] Compared to other industrialized democracies, such as the United Kingdom, France, or Germany, American labor law and practice is outside the mainstream.

Germany is described by Freedom House as having a "system of protections for workers' rights and workplace condition . . . among the strongest in the world. Freedom of association is protected in law and in practice, the majority of employees are covered by collective-bargaining agreements, and unions play an important role in the country's democracy."[40] Thomas Geoghegan notes that, in addition to strong labor laws, German workers are protected and empowered through a social democratic system built on works councils, co-determined boards of directors, and regional wage-setting institutions.[41] These "three big building blocks of German social democracy" in effect free the unions to bargain on a macro level with employer federations.[42] Under such a system, even if labor unions are attacked or weakened, workers have other structural safeguards that approximate some of the protections unions often ensure. Ironically, this pro-worker system was largely set up by Dwight Eisenhower and other Americans in Germany following World War II.[43]

France similarly has a strong, protected, and free labor movement. Freedom House finds: "Workers do not face pressure by the government or employers to join or not to join certain trade unions. Strikes are a constitutional right with minimal regulation, and they occur frequently. Nevertheless, some employers attempt to weaken trade union activity through tactics such as dividing enterprises into smaller units or outsourcing. Antiunion propaganda in large enterprises can be a problem."[44] Overall, Freedom House reports that in France: "Workers' right to organize in unions is protected, and trade unions remain strong, although membership has declined over the past two decades. Trade unions can operate without interference or control by the government and political parties."[45] While France has a relatively low union density rate, most workers are nevertheless covered by union collective bargaining agreements. Due to the different legal and political status unions in other countries enjoy, most other industrialized democracies have much greater union coverage than they do actual membership.[46] For example, the Center for Economic Policy Research (CEPR) found that in 2007 membership in unions in France stood at approximately 10 percent, while the level of worker coverage by a union remained at 90 percent.[47] Under these conditions of minimal government and business interference, and consistent levels of coverage, union membership can expand and contract without leading to the vast economic inequalities found in America.

In the United Kingdom, Freedom House finds "workers' right to organize in unions is protected."[48] Workers in the United Kingdom enjoy a level of freedom to join or not join a union unimaginable in the United States, and the complaints made by unions or the ILO about the abridgment of these rights are minor in comparison to those found in the United States. Freedom House reports:

> Workers do not face pressure from the government or employers to join or not join certain trade unions. There are some restrictions on strikes that are criticized by unions, including measures that outlaw sympathy strikes and limit strikes to employment-related matters. . . . Laws in effect since 2005 prohibit union-busting tactics by employers. Collective bargaining takes place, generally at the level of the enterprise. Although collective-bargaining agreements are honored in practice, in 2006 the International Labour Organization expressed concern that Britain does not grant unions the right to gain access to workplaces.[49]

Germany, France, and the United Kingdom represent only three examples of comparators from Western Europe that have less hostile public and private environments for unionization, and far greater protections for workers whose labor rights are infringed. Other countries, such as Canada, Belize, or Uruguay, could similarly be offered as examples to show more conducive environments for workers in America's own backyard. Even a significant number of countries in the former Soviet Union can be shown to have better protections for workers exercising their labor rights.[50]

Like Freedom House, Human Rights Watch has found that the United States' laws and practice concerning labor rights are outside the norm:

> The U.S. prohibition on solidarity action contrasts sharply with practice of most other countries and runs counter to principles developed by the ILO's Committee on Freedom of Association over many decades of treating cases under Conventions 87 and 98. . . . In the European Union (EU), all member states except the United Kingdom recognize the lawfulness of workers' solidarity action. At the same time, they regulate such action to minimize its effects and to channel disputes toward peaceful resolutions.[51]

In another report, Human Rights Watch suggested, "In the United States, labor law enforcement efforts often fail to deter unlawful conduct. When the law is applied, enervating delays and weak remedies invite continued violations."[52]

With regard to protections for organizing, the United States has lagged behind Western European democracies for several decades, and now is starting to lag behind new democracies as well. John Logan, research director of the Institute for Research on Labor Employment at the University of California–Berkeley has found that "workers in these [emerging democracies] can gain bargaining coverage without having to endure management-dominated representation elections and bargaining campaigns, as they must do in the United States."[53]

Legal scholar Theodore J. St. Antoine recognized twenty-five years ago the "keen irony" behind the fact that American corporations and government stand out as among the most anti-union, because America has some of the most corporate and government-friendly unions in the world. "Ours is the most conservative, least ideological of all labor movements, traditionally committed to the capitalistic system and to the principle that management should have the primary responsibility for managing. Yet employers will pay millions of dollars to experts in 'union avoidance' in order to maintain their nonunion status."[54] There is a further irony that, while American workers face from employers what St. Antoine describes as an "intensity of opposition to unionization" that "has no parallel in the western industrialized world,"[55] the government is perhaps among the most lax in the western industrialized world in protecting workers. In the country where private opposition to unionization is greatest, there should be proportionate public protections. However, American labor laws make it harder for employees to organize and offer few protections from intransigent employers.[56] Freedom House finds: "The United States today . . . —unlike most European countries—features an overall political environment that is distinctly hostile to unions, collective bargaining, and labor protest."[57] In other industrialized democracies, there is nothing akin to the union-busting industry that exists in America. "Among developed democracies, the United States is alone in having a sophisticated industry worth hundreds of millions of dollars per year devoted entirely to helping management resist collective bargaining."[58]

Freedom House recognizes that unions in the United States enjoy a fair number of *de jure* protections, but it criticizes the failure of these protections to deter wrongdoing and the lack of political will to protect unions.

> Management has used a variety of tactics to block unionization, including the intimidation of union activists. . . . For example, they illegally threaten to close a plant or facility in the event of unionization, and ignore laws against harassing or dismissing union activists. Workers are typically unable to obtain timely justice for acts of reprisal by management; it takes an average of two years for a worker to win reinstatement or compensation after a finding of illegal dismissal for union activity. Furthermore, when found guilty by the courts or the NLRB, companies are often compelled to do nothing more than provide back pay, a slap-on-the-wrist penalty that has little deterrent effect. Even when unionization has occurred, employers frequently negotiate with labor representatives in bad faith, engaging in collective bargaining without any intention of reaching a contract.[59]

While America receives low ranking in labor rights, Freedom House praises the strength of American anti-discrimination laws and the corresponding legal remedies.

> Like other established democracies, the United States has a complex network of laws, policies, and enforcement agencies designed to monitor the employment sector for evidence of discrimination based on race, gender, ethnicity, or age. Antidiscrimination laws are fortified by a series of court decisions that bolster the power of government to prosecute cases of workplace bias. And there are laws that make it possible for employees to sue corporations or government agencies in cases of wrongful dismissal.[60]

The anti-discrimination laws in America show a deep respect for the dignity of the individual at work. They treat discriminatory conduct as antithetical to American values and the practice of democracy. Unfortunately, American labor law stops short of protecting workers from discrimination in the practice of their rights of association, and allows these types of discrimination to proceed largely unhindered. In doing so, America places itself outside international norms, and in league with countries with repressive political regimes. And the American worker finds herself more fiercely attacked and less protected than a worker in almost any other industrialized democracy.

CHAPTER FIVE

The Legislative Proposal
Amending the Civil Rights Act for Labor Organizing

We have argued throughout this book that the Civil Rights Act should be amended to protect labor organizing. But how would labor rights be administered and resolved under the Civil Rights Act? Would the National Labor Relations Board (NLRB) continue to administer the disputes involving labor, or the Equal Employment Opportunity Commission (EEOC)? How would agricultural workers, supervisors, and public employees—all of whom are covered by the Civil Rights Act but not the NLRA—be treated? If there is a civil right to join a union, should there also be a civil right not to join a union? In this chapter, we propose a model statute and seek to answer these questions.

Our central thesis is that a false and damaging legal distinction exists between the fields of labor law and employment law that makes each field far less effective than it should be, and leaves many victims of illegal employment practices without adequate relief. To an outsider—one not steeped in the history and development of these areas—the distinction would seem bizarre and counterproductive. An employee who has suffered arbitrary or discriminatory treatment at work would quickly realize that this artificial demarcation in employment law makes it much more difficult, and sometimes impossible, for her to seek relief. The false separation of these areas of law does not simply make them more complicated for the employee who has been wronged, and cannot articulate her employer's exact motive; it hinders the explicit goals of each area by not allowing these naturally complementing facets to be used to protect the employee's rights at work.

Employment discrimination law and labor law each set a floor beneath which society has labeled employer's private conduct a public wrong. Both of these legal structures implicate fundamental American values of equal protection and freedoms of association and speech, protected by the U.S. Constitution.[1] However, only one of these areas—employment discrimination law—is currently protected as a civil right, with all the attendant processes and remedies. Ultimately, this legal distinction's greatest harm is that it has permitted the wholesale exclusion from the protections afforded civil rights of a broad swath of illegal employment practices.

Overview of Labor and Discrimination Law in America

Statutory law is the sole source of relief for most American workers who have suffered some adverse employment action by their employer. The default rule for most American workers is the rule of at-will employment,[2] which the courts have succinctly paraphrased as the employer's right to terminate an employee for "good reason, bad reason, or no reason at all."[3] Since most nonunionized employees do not have contracts that provide supplementary protections, they must turn to statutory protections to vindicate their rights at work. For most private sector employees, the universe of these protections includes only state and federal employment discrimination laws and state and federal labor laws.[4]

As we noted earlier, the primary labor law statutes that protect employees from adverse employment actions based on "concerted activity" are the National Labor Relations Act, (NLRA) which covers certain categories of private sector employees; the Railway Labor Act (RLA),[5] which covers certain transportation workers such as railway and airline employees; and a host of public sector laws that cover some state and federal employees. Most of these public sector labor laws seek to protect the broad right encapsulated in Section 7 of the NLRA that prohibits an employer from taking adverse employment action against an employee for exercising her right "to self-organization, to form, join, or assist labor organizations, to bargain collectively through representatives of their own choosing, and to engage in other concerted activities for the purpose of collective bargaining or other mutual aid or protection."[6]

Title VII of the Civil Rights Act, and the state and local statutes modeled on Title VII, provide the bulk of protections in the employment law arena.[7] Title VII prohibits employers from terminating, disciplining, or taking employment actions "because of such individual's race, color, religion, sex, or national origin."[8] Subsequently, additional federal statutes have been passed that have supplemented the original protected categories. These include, but are not limited to: the Age Discrimination in Employment Act of 1967 (ADEA), which prohibits employment discrimination against persons forty years of age or older;[9] the Pregnancy Discrimination Act of 1978, which prohibits discrimination based on pregnancy, childbirth, or related conditions;[10] Titles I and V of the American with Disabilities Act of 1990 (ADA), which prohibits employment discrimination against qualified individuals based upon disability or perceived disability;[11] the Uniformed Services Employment and Reemployment Rights Act of 1994 (USERRA), which prohibits discrimination based on "membership, application for membership, performance of service, application for service, or obligation" with a "uniformed service";[12] Title II of the Genetic Information Nondiscrimination Act of 2008 (GINA), which prohibits employment discrimination based on genetic information about the individual,[13] and laws prohibiting discrimination based upon indebtedness or bankruptcy.[14]

Many state and local statutes mirror the federal regulations, and several have added additional categories of protections. These include laws prohibiting employment discrimination based upon prior criminal conviction,[15] sexual orientation,[16] "use or nonuse of lawful products off the employer's premises during nonworking hours,"[17] "honorably discharged veteran or military status,"[18] and on the basis of an employee declining to attend or participate in employer-sponsored meeting about religious or political matters.[19]

These state and local statutes offer another set of avenues for adding protections for the right to organize. However, these statutes are less preferable than the federal solution proposed here, for a number of reasons. First, federal preemption doctrine precludes states from passing laws that conflict with federal laws.[20] The current Supreme Court has taken a broad view of this doctrine, and state civil rights statutes that protect an individual's right to organize may be struck down by the federal courts because they would be preempted by the NLRA.[21] Second, state labor laws are less stable than federal labor laws, as can be witnessed by the recent radical shifts in public sector labor laws throughout the country.[22] Lastly, the NLRA sought to set a national policy for labor law, and this intent would be best served by a national approach to reform.

Based on a literal reading of the statutory text, the prohibited employer conduct under the NLRA is perhaps broader than the conduct prohibited under Title VII, as Title VII only prohibits adverse employment actions such as hiring, firing, disciplining, or actions based on harassment or hostile work environments,[23] whereas the NLRA prohibits the ostensibly broader conduct of interfering, restraining, or coercing employees in exercising their rights to organize or "other concerted activities for the purpose of collective bargaining or other mutual aid or protection."[24] Despite the seemingly broader protections under the NLRA, the procedures and remedies of each statute have made Title VII hugely successful in reducing overt discrimination in the workplace, while the NLRA has been an abject failure in promoting an equality of power between the employee and employer through organization and collective bargaining.

In order to understand how two statutes that each protect fundamental rights of employees could diverge so greatly with regard to efficacy, it is necessary to examine the processes an individual employee must follow under each statute and the remedies available to her, should she be successful. This comparative analysis will illustrate why employment discrimination law has been successful where labor law has failed, and why labor law should be reconceived under the civil rights rubric alongside what is currently considered employment discrimination law.

The Current Processes: The National Labor Relations Act and the Civil Rights Act, Compared

Currently, if an employee suffers an adverse employment action, such as termination, suspension, demotion, harassment, reduction in pay or hours, or the like, and she feels it is due to her membership in a protected class *or* due to her attempt to organize or join a union or engage in other protected activities, she must file a charge with a federal agency. If the discriminatory reason is due to her membership in a protected class of race, color, religion, sex, national origin, age, or disability, then she must file her charge with the EEOC, with limited exceptions for Equal Pay Act claims and Section 1981 claims based in contractual relationships. If the discriminatory reason stems from her union or concerted activity, then she must file her charge with the NLRB.

The National Labor Relations Board Process

Under the current NLRB model, if an employee or union (or employer) suffers from an unfair labor practice (ULP), that party must file a charge with the regional director of the NLRB.[25] The local office of the NLRB conducts an investigation, and if it concludes that there is merit to the claim, it files a complaint against the party allegedly committing the ULP (usually the employer).[26] The NLRB may also refuse to issue a complaint if it finds that there is not enough evidence to sustain a complaint. If the NLRB chooses not to file a complaint, the aggrieved party may appeal to the general counsel, but has no private remedies.[27] The decision of the general counsel is final, and no matter the wrongs suffered by the employee, the agency is often the only route to relief.[28]

If the regional director files a complaint, then a hearing is conducted before an administrative law judge (ALJ), where the NLRB (not the employee or union) is the prosecuting party.[29] The aggrieved party may have counsel at the hearing and supplement the NLRB's prosecution, but the matter is in the hands of the NLRB. A hearing at the NLRB does not allow most forms of pre-trial discovery, which has the effect of limiting the scope of the case that can be made against the employer.[30] Without broad discovery, the hearing consists almost entirely of witnesses, public information, and information and documents that the employer volunteers. This restriction not only weakens any possible case against the employer, but it also factors into the employer's calculus when choosing whether to commit an unfair labor practice. Parties fear litigation not only because of the ultimate remedies that they may have to pay, but also because of the burdensome process of litigation. Discovery constitutes at least a several-months process consisting of document production, answering interrogatories, submitting to depositions, and having to admit or deny broad categories of inquiry. The standard for discovery is quite liberal. Under the Federal Rules of Procedure, "relevant information need not be admissible at the trial if the discovery appears reasonably calculated to lead to the discovery of admissible evidence."[31] In effect, the discovery process is an enormous burden on the defendant in a lawsuit because it permits the plaintiff to have broad access to an employer's files, employees, and evidence, with the goal of bringing transparency and fairness to the process.

The ALJ's order is not self-enforcing, and the parties may accept the order and choose to comply, or either party may file exceptions to the five-member, presidentially appointed board, which will issue a final order.[32] These five members—three from the president's political party and two from the opposing party—sitting as a body in Washington, D.C., are tasked with issuing final orders for almost every category of private sector labor dispute in the county that is excepted by one of the parties involved. The board order is also not self-enforcing; rather, the prevailing party must seek enforcement from a federal court of appeals. Some have found a growing unfamiliarity with the highly technical area of labor law among court of appeals judges, which is leading to problems at the enforcement stage.[33]

This lengthy NLRB process is the only venue available to an employee discriminated against for union activity because many private rights of action that might otherwise be available to her are preempted by the NLRA.[34] According to the 2009 NLRB Annual Report, the median age of a case pending board decision was 963 days old.[35] Following this nearly three-year administrative process, an employer can simply ignore the board's final order, and the NLRB must seek enforcement from a federal court of appeals. Due to the lack of discovery and meager remedies, employers often have little incentive to settle cases, especially those employers that have willfully broken the law in order to keep the union out of the workplace. In such instances, the more time the case drags on, the better for the employer, because it propounds a sense in the workplace that the employer can flout federal labor law without consequence.

The Equal Employment Opportunity Commission Process

On the surface, the administrative process at the EEOC is in many respects similar to the NLRB administrative process. Indeed, the EEOC was partly modeled on the NLRB, and all hearings and investigations conducted by the EEOC are governed by section 161 of the NLRA, which governs the NLRB process.[36]

Strictly speaking, there is nothing inherently superior about the EEOC administrative process, as compared to the NLRB administrative process. Few who deal with the agency laud it as a model of efficiency or the paradigm of a strong agency. The EEOC is infamous for its ongoing backlog of cases, which often hinders the agency in effectively handling new charges. According to the 2010 EEOC annual report, the agency had an intake of 93,277 new private-sector discrimination charges, and completed 2009 with a backlog of 86,338 charges.[37]

Having said that, there are several important differences between the administrative process under Title VII as compared to the administrative process under the NLRA. The first is that under Title VII, the employee may opt out. Though Title VII requires an employee to file a charge with the EEOC, the employee may request a "notice of right to sue" from the agency anytime after 180 days have passed.[38] This right to sue letter provides the employee a private right of action in federal court for ninety days after its issuance.

Title VII not only provides the right to sue the employer, it also provides the means and the incentive. First, based upon the plaintiff's financial ability to retain counsel, her failed efforts to retain counsel, and whether the plaintiff presents a meritorious claim, the court may appoint counsel.[39] At the district court's discretion, any one of these factors may be determinative.[40] In addition to providing employees the opportunity to obtain court-appointed counsel,[41] Title VII provides that a prevailing party is entitled to attorneys' fees and costs.[42] This provision recognizes the fact that many employees who suffer employment discrimination are economically unable to finance the necessary litigation to vindicate their rights, and that society's interests in ending discriminatory practices weighs in favor of this exception to the so-called "American rule" that each litigant, win or lose, pays her own way.[43] Furthermore, the availability of attorneys' fees and costs has created a strong bar of employment attorneys that are willing and able to take employment discrimination suits on a contingency basis, often with no up-front costs or retainers.

The availability of attorneys' fees has created the possibility for many employees to bring suit, but the difficulties of litigation extend beyond the costs involved. Litigating an employment suit may involve a multi-year process of making public the private areas of one's life, involving one's friends and former coworkers, expending a great deal of time and emotional energy in preparation, and going up against an adversary who is invariably larger, richer, and has more resources. One's credibility is questioned at every turn, and there is an abiding fear that the litigation will lead to the plaintiff being labeled an overly sensitive "problem" employee that no future employer will want to hire. Therefore, even with attorneys' fees accounted for, many aggrieved employees would forego the process of litigation if the remedies did not go a long way toward making them whole.

The Supreme Court has stated that "[Title VII] is intended to make victims of employment discrimination whole, and the attainment of this objective requires that the persons aggrieved . . . be so far as possible, restored to the position where they would have been were it not for the unlawful discrimination."[44] To this end, a successful plaintiff may be awarded a variety of remedies, including back pay (with interest), reinstatement or front pay, equitable relief, compensatory damages, and punitive damages.[45]

Back pay includes not only salary loss, but also lost overtime, shift differentials, health and pension benefits, and fringe benefits, with the total amount of back pay presumptively calculated with prejudgment interest.[46] The back pay award is mitigated by "interim earnings" that the plaintiff earns between being terminated and final disposition of the case,[47] but these interim earnings do not include government benefits, such as unemployment compensation, Social Security, welfare, or the like.[48] An employer may limit its liability with regard to back pay by unconditionally offering the plaintiff the job she was terminated from or denied.[49] Unless there is "excessive hostility" between the parties, a plaintiff may not be awarded back pay going forward from the moment she has received such an unconditional offer for reinstatement, regardless of whether she accepts the offer.[50]

A successful plaintiff is also entitled to reinstatement at her previous position or, if that is impossible or inappropriate because of the nature of the discrimination, she will be awarded front pay in an amount equal to what she would have earned if not for the unlawful discrimination.[51] Front pay consists of continuing future economic losses resulting from the unlawful discrimination, as opposed to the back pay awards that seek to make the plaintiff whole as of the date of judgment. Significant awards of front pay are usually awarded to plaintiffs in age-discrimination suits because one of the main factors that the court considers in calculating such awards is the comparable employment opportunities for an individual in the plaintiff's position. With older plaintiffs closer to retirement age, there are fewer comparable employment opportunities, and less time to pursue those opportunities prior to retirement.

In addition to providing lost wages and benefits, Title VII recognizes the toll that losing one's job has on an individual, and seeks to restore the individual fully while also punishing employers that engage in intentional discrimination. For this reason, Title VII permits a court to award compensatory and punitive damages.[52] Compensatory damages includes future pecuniary losses and money damages to cover emotional pain, suffering, inconvenience, mental anguish, loss of enjoyment of life, injury to professional standing, injury to character and reputation, injury to credit standing, loss of health, and other nonpecuniary losses.[53] This is necessary because losing one's job substantially affects every other part of the individual's life, and these effects often cascade and become worse with time.

Furthermore, if the employer is not a government or political subdivision, the plaintiff may be entitled to punitive damages if she can demonstrate that "the respondent engaged in a discriminatory practice or discriminatory practices with malice or with reckless indifference to the federally protected rights of an aggrieved individual."[54] The combined total compensatory and punitive damages that an employee may receive follows a step scale based on the number of employees employed, and has been capped at $300,000.[55]

Along with the remedies and private right of action available under Title VII, plaintiffs have two procedural rights that seem unextraordinary in litigation, but are unavailable to the employee bringing a charge under the NLRA: the right to a jury trial and the right to full discovery. The right to a jury stems from the availability of compensatory and punitive damages, which only a jury can award.[56] Defendants in employment discrimination suits fear the jury trial, viewing it as a "negative lottery," where "when they lose, they can lose big."[57] Employers view juries as unpredictable in their assignment of liability (and the value of such liability), and juries often relate more to the aggrieved employee over the economically motivated employer.[58] Therefore, many employers try hard to have the matter disposed of on summary judgment or are amenable to pretrial settlements.

The other procedural right available to the parties is discovery. Because employment discrimination suits are brought in federal court, the Federal Rules of Civil Procedure govern. Under these rules, parties are entitled to a range of pretrial discovery, including depositions, interrogatories, requests for production of documents, and requests for admissions.[59] Courts recognize that a plaintiff's case under Title VII will usually involve a great deal of circumstantial evidence, so as a general rule, courts will allow a broad scope of discovery. This will often require the employer to reveal information regarding its past employment practices, its financials, lists of possible witnesses, and other internal data. Though discovery is available to both parties, it is a facet of litigation that bears a much heavier burden on the defendant in employment cases. On principled grounds, some employers hate the idea of employees being able to have access to so many aspects of the business. Beyond this, there are the internal and legal costs associated with being on the receiving end of discovery requests. Each answer and each document is usually collected using internal resources, and then scrutinized and reconstructed by legal counsel, placing several layers of costs on an employer.

These procedures and remedies seek to make the plaintiff whole after suffering discriminatory treatment, but they also have a secondary effect of serving as a significant deterrent to employers. American employers spend significant time and money training management and employees about the rules under Title VII, so as not to be the subject of litigation. As a result, there is far less overt discrimination in the American workplace as a matter of policy. Though employers and managers still engage in discriminatory practices, Title VII has greatly reduced the severity and scope of such practices.[60] Title VII serves as one of the few instances where legislation has changed culture. As Thomas Geoghegan notes, "The Jim Crow law creates one kind of culture, and the Civil Rights Act over time creates another."[61]

The NLRA versus the Civil Rights Act, in Practice

Using one telling example, Harvard law professor Benjamin Sachs vividly illustrates the different remedial regimes under the NLRA and Title VII for the same discriminatory conduct.[62] The documented case involved a group of Latino construction workers in Colorado who were treated like second-class employees by the company, Phase II, as compared to their Anglo counterparts on the jobsite:

> According to affidavits . . . supervisors routinely referred to Mexican immigrant workers in viciously derogatory terms. Workers alleged, for example, that daily work meetings were punctuated with remarks including, "Hey . . . wetbacks," and that managers would berate workers with the Spanish phrase "muevete mojados," or "move it, wetbacks." Mexican workers on the Fitzsimmons project also were compelled to use different, and dirtier, lavatory facilities than their Anglo coworkers. Thus, "when [Phase II] Mexican workers attempted to use the cleaner ground floor restrooms, the foreman would call them 'flojos' [lazy], reprimand them for taking too much time, and deny them the key."
>
> Likewise, Phase II supervisors provided drinking water to Anglo workers but not the Mexican workers. During morning work meetings, "the supervisors told the Mexican workers that the water was not for them, but only for them, pointing to the Anglo workers who stood apart from the Mexican workers." And, eventually, "the supervisors placed the drinking water in their trailer, where

the Anglo workers could enter and drink, but where the Mexican workers were not allowed." Finally, Phase II supervisors made elevators on the worksite available to Anglo employees but denied Mexican workers access to the elevators, even when Mexican workers were transporting heavy work materials. Indeed, Mexican workers "were reprimanded by foremen when they were seen waiting for [the elevator]."[63]

The employees could have pursued a claim under Title VII for discrimination based on national origin, but they wanted to form a union and engage in collective bargaining to vindicate their rights. In response to this attempt to organize, the employer threatened the workforce, targeted union organizers with paycuts, and stole personal property of organizers.[64]

The employees filed a charge with the NLRB alleging violations of their rights to organize. The NLRA does not speak to the specific employment violations that these employees suffered, but it does prevent employer retaliation based on the employees' attempt to organize. Though section 8(a)(1) and 8(a)(3) of the NLRA specifically prohibit such retaliatory conduct, the NLRB chose not to issue a complaint.[65] On appeal, the NLRB proposed a settlement under which the employer would pay no damages, but rather have to post a notice "informing employees of their NLRA rights and announcing, inter alia, that '[w]e will not threaten our employees with loss of their jobs because they choose to engage in a protected concerted work stoppage.'"[66] Such notices usually consist of the following language:

FEDERAL LAW GIVES YOU THE RIGHT TO
- Form, join or assist a union
- Choose representatives to bargain with us on your behalf
- Act together with other employees for your benefit and protection
- Choose not to engage in any of these protected activities.[67]

The notice must be posted "in 'conspicuous' places, including *all* places where notices to employees or members are customarily posted."[68]

The workers responded by going to the EEOC to file a charge for the discriminatory treatment. The EEOC investigated and found violations of Title VII because the workers were organizing in order to assert their right not to be discriminated against due to national origin.[69] The EEOC brought suit, which resulted in a consent decree.

Pursuant to the decree, the company agreed to pay $750,000 in damages: $600,000 to the ten charging parties and an additional $150,000 to other eligible class members. The decree also mandated that [the company] implement an equal employment opportunity training program for all managerial employees. Finally, [the company] was enjoined from future acts of retaliation for employee activity protected by Title VII, thus subjecting the company to contempt sanctions should it again interfere with workers' collective action designed to combat workplace discrimination.[70]

This story is telling. It illustrates well how the same retaliatory conduct by an employer is resolved through two agencies tasked with protecting employees. The NLRB could offer these employees little, and was no deterrent toward the company. Its solution was to require the company to post notice so that the employees knew their rights. However, the employees already knew their rights, which is precisely why they took action to organize a union, and why they filed a charge with the NLRB. In this example, it was shown that President Franklin D. Roosevelt's goal of the NLRA insuring and promoting "economic advance and common justice"[71] was failing because it was without the tools to achieve even the most basic protections. What the NLRB process showed was that these were essentially rights without a remedy.

On the other hand, the EEOC process, which included the EEOC bringing suit on the employees' behalf, led to meaningful relief. The consent decree provided not only for payment of damages to aggrieved employees, but also provided two forms of injunctive relief in order to curb future abuses: the managerial training program attempted to use education on unlawful employment practices in the hopes that knowledge of the employees' rights would promote appropriate managerial conduct, while the injunction against future retaliation provided the employees a route to speedy resolution should the court be ignored.

Sachs provides this account as one example where employees and attorneys can use employment law to vindicate labor rights. He acknowledges up front the fact that this approach can only be used in certain limited situations.[72] This approach of circumventing labor law by couching the complaint in terms of Title VII is likely the best that can be achieved under the current legal regimes; however, it cannot effectuate the broad goals of national labor policy.

The Failure of the NLRA

As we outlined in chapter 3, the ineffectiveness of the NLRA has been known for some time, and has been well-documented.[73] In 1984, the House Subcommittee on Labor-Management Relations conducted hearings and released a report entitled "The Failure of Labor Law—A Betrayal of American Workers," in which it pronounced that the NLRA "has ceased to accomplish its purpose."[74] Similarly, Harvard law professor Paul Weiler stated that "[c]ontemporary American labor law more and more resembles an elegant tombstone for a dying institution."[75] The decline of labor in America has not abated since the 1980s, when these pronouncements were made, and not a year goes by without a labor historian or scholar bemoaning labor's slow death.[76]

Several years ago, the chairwoman of the NLRB, Wilma B. Liebman, summarized the view held by many, writing:

> Various commentators describe the National Labor Relations Act . . . as dead, dying, or at least "largely irrelevant to the contemporary workplace"—a doomed legal dinosaur. In their view, the Act has failed to protect workers' rights to organize and to promote the institution of collective bargaining. Scholars contend that labor law suffers from "ossification." Some even say that it is "contributing to the demise of the very rights it was enacted to protect." Collective action seems "moribund." Supporters of the Act are "in despair." The National Labor Relations Board, charged with administering the Act, is "isolated and politicized." "What went wrong?" and "Can we fix it?" are the questions of the day.[77]

Various approaches have been recommended to create a labor law regime that truly protects the rights of employees to self-organize and collectively bargain over the terms and conditions of their employment, but none has proven successful in even navigating through the legislative process. Some have advocated revising the NLRA,[78] but even minor revisions that simply sought to slow the decline of labor have failed in the legislative process.[79] Some have advocated abandoning the NLRA as a defective document that does more harm than good, and suggest promulgating a new stronger statute.[80] However, labor law is one of the most contentious issues in Congress, and corporations have shown willingness to expend great sums of money to defeat even modest changes, making reforming the NLRA an extremely difficult process.[81]

It is unlikely that in the political climate of the foreseeable future, any stronger set of labor regulations could be passed by the federal government. One of the most interesting approaches has been one proposed by Sachs, which he has termed "employment law as labor law" and which requires no lobbying and legislative effort, because it represents a sort of grass-roots process of labor law reform that exploits the natural overlaps with employment law.[82] Sachs describes the ongoing inability of labor law to provide meaningful relief in mechanical terms, and describes how this has led to the turn to employment law:

> The deep dysfunctionality of the NLRA constitutes a blockage only of the traditional legal channel for collective action and labor-management relations. Because workers, unions, and certain employers continue to demand collective organization and interaction, this blockage has led not to "ossification" but to a hydraulic effect: unable to find an outlet through the NLRA, the pressure from this continuing demand for collective action has forced open alternative legal channels.
>
> . . . Faced with a traditional labor law regime that has proven ineffectual, workers and their lawyers are turning to employment statutes like the Fair Labor Standards Act (FLSA) and Title VII of the Civil Rights Act of 1964 as the legal guardians of their efforts to organize and act collectively. Workers, that is, are relying on employment statutes, not only for the traditional purpose of securing the substantive rights provided by those laws, but also as the legal architecture that facilitates their organizational and collective activity—a legal architecture we conventionally call labor law.[83]

Sachs is describing one way—exemplified above by the Phase II employees—in which the artificial distinctions between labor and employment law are being deconstructed by ingenious attorneys and employees. However, the possible scope of this approach is admittedly limited to certain situations and it would be far superior to simply shift labor discrimination into the general category of employment discrimination law.[84]

In describing the arc of the NLRA's rise and decline, Liebman stated: "For several decades, the labor law regime worked, and so it was respected. The law seemed to promise, and to some extent delivered, workplace democracy and equality in bargaining power."[85] Today, however, the NLRA, does not work in promoting workplace democracy and equality in bargaining power, so it is not respected and is often simply disregarded. Writing recently about Boeing's public threats to move a plant to South Carolina—a "right to work state"—as payback for a strike, Thomas Geoghegan expressed surprise that the CEO of a major corporation would so openly violate the NLRA: "The Boeing case may show that labor is so out of mind that CEOs have forgotten what they can or cannot say. It would have been easy enough for Boeing to move the production line to South Carolina and let the workers in Seattle draw the conclusion. There is little bar to a runaway shop if the CEO is careful with his public statements."[86]

Minor changes to the NLRA cannot restore the act, and in its current state, Liebman is left in the position of having to argue that the board "can play a modest but meaningful role in preserving the values of this Act and in furthering its aims" rather than conceding to the alternative of "operat[ing] on the legal margins of a failed statute."[87] This range of alternatives falls far short of Roosevelt's desire to create legislation that insures "economic advance and common justice."

A Model Statute

This complicated, and seemingly intractable, problem may be addressed by simply tearing down the artificial distinction between labor and employment rights. In effect, this would reorient the basic right to join a union from a collective right to an individual right, and place labor and employment discrimination on a similar plane in the eyes of the law by treating both as violations of the individual's civil rights. It would not require the breaking of any new legal ground, as labor discrimination has been illegal for over seventy-five years; it would simply place the prohibitions and protections under a stronger statute. The legal mechanism for achieving this result is the amendment of the Civil Rights Act to include protection for an employee to join or not join a union. A statute making such changes could take a variety of forms, but the following model amendments are offered as an example of a simple bill that could radically alter labor law in America, by finally acknowledging that the opportunity to organize or join a union is a civil right. The following is a model statute and a brief analysis of the functions of the important provisions:

> *Section 1:* No employer shall restrain, coerce or interfere with an employee's right to join a labor union, or engage in any act or act of reprisal which has the effect of restraining, coercing or interfering

with an employee's decision to support, oppose or take any other position with respect to union membership.

Section 2: The district court shall issue injunctions (including preliminary injunctions) to redress any violation of Section 1, or reinstate the employee or provide any other appropriate injunctive relief on behalf of the affected employee or similarly situated employees.

Section 3: The district court shall grant full legal fees and costs to any employee who obtains any significant relief and in awarding the appropriate hourly rate the district court shall take into account the use of the hourly rate of the employer's lawyer as the lodestar for such determination.

Section 4: Sections 703(a)(1), 703(a)(2), 703(b), 703(c)(1), 703(c)(2), 703(d), 703(e) of the Revised Statutes (42 U.S.C. 2000e-2) are amended by inserting "on the basis of seeking union membership," after "sex,".

Section 5: The employee shall be entitled to all other relief provided under the Civil Rights Act of 1991, including back pay, compensatory, and punitive damages.

Section 6: All actions brought pursuant to Section 1, other than Section 2 injunctions, shall be filed and handled by the National Labor Relations Board and proceed under procedures established for the Equal Employment Opportunity Commission (29 C.F.R. 1601 et seq.).

Section 7: The Secretary of Labor shall be entitled to bring an action on behalf of any employee who has suffered a loss of rights under Section 1.

Section 8: No employer shall be liable to any employee for punitive damages for any violation of Section 1 during such period as the employer has entered a collective bargaining agreement with an employee representative or labor organization or has entered an agreement in good faith to use a third party arbitrator to determine the terms of an appropriate collective bargaining agreement in the event that the employer and employee representative fail to reach an agreement.[88]

This statute would effectively shift the basic right of an employee to join or organize a union from what has long been conceived of as a collective right to an individual right. This reconception does not transform all labor rights into individual rights, but rather recognizes that when an employee takes action in joining or organizing a union, there is not yet a collective framework that can protect her. Solidarity and organization are being constructed in this initial phase, and if the individual employee is targeted, her individual rights are infringed. The model statute above recognizes the individual nature of early stage union organizing, and provides prohibitions and protections for the individual so that she can proceed to assert collective demands and enforce those through the collective mechanisms.

Section 4 of the model statute provides the crux of the amendment, by making it unlawful for an employer to terminate, discipline, or take other employment actions because of such individual's race, color, religion, sex, on the basis of seeking union membership, or national origin. The addition of these seven words—"on the basis of seeking union membership"—would provide real protections for a right promised in 1935 of granting employees the right to associate, organize, and have a voice in their employment and economic standing. These words would finally destroy the artificial and untenable distinction between employment rights and labor rights, and acknowledge that both are in significant part based on individual rights. These words would usher in an acknowledgment that a violation of certain basic individual rights of employees, whether based on the employee's attendance at a religious meeting or a union meeting, should be prohibited. Only organizational rights are protected here, rather than all concerted activities, because it is during organizational efforts that the individual employee would benefit most from the individual rights model without abrogating her collective labor rights.[89]

Section 1 of the model statute imports the restrictions from Section 8(a)(1) of the NLRA against employer interference with an employee's right to join a union. It also imports the provision's no proof of discriminatory intent requirement by prohibiting the conduct, without regard to whether the employer was acting in good faith.[90] The Supreme Court has stated that there are strong policy reasons for looking at the effect of the employer's conduct, rather than its motives:

> Otherwise the protected activity would lose some of its immunity, since the example of employees who are discharged on false charges would or might have a deterrent effect on other employees. Union activity often engenders strong emotions and gives rise to active rumors. A protected activity acquires a precarious status if innocent employees can be discharged while engaging in it, even though the employer acts in good faith.[91]

Sections 2, 3, and 5 of the model statute work to fully integrate labor rights into the Civil Rights Act. Section 2 removes from the arsenal of the employer the ability to quash a budding labor movement by simply harassing, coercing, or firing the employees that are central to the organization effort. Though illegal under the NLRA, employers often engage in this practice because other employees quickly understand the implicit message that if they step up to organize they too will be punished. As outlined above, under the current labor law regime, employees fired for joining or organizing a union can seek redress in the form of reinstatement and mitigated back pay (without interest). If they are successful, they will receive these remedies within two to three years. The employer, whether successful or not at the NLRB, will have successfully kept out the union. Under Section 2 of the model statute, an employee fired for organizing a union could seek a preliminary injunction for reinstatement, and thereby return to work within a few days in order to preserve the status quo. Other employees will quickly understand the message of such injunctive action: that the courts will prevent an employer from attempting to punish them for exercising their civil rights. In time, employers too will realize the uselessness of attacking an organizer, and will likely cease this unlawful, but currently quite effective, tactic. This type of injunctive relief has proven very effective under the Railway Labor Act.[92]

Section 3 serves a variety of purposes. First and foremost, it makes full recovery of attorneys' fees and costs mandatory at the hourly rate of management side attorneys, even if there is less than complete success in the litigation. This provision will not only insure that employees are able to secure representation on a contingency arrangement, it will also help to build the ranks of plaintiff-side labor attorneys. As the labor movement has declined, so have the ranks of union-side labor attorneys. Beyond the union legal departments, there are fewer and fewer attorneys that practice and understand traditional labor law, and providing statutory attorneys' fees will help rebuild a strong bar of such skilled attorneys. This section would also help fund the sort of litigation strategy developed by the NAACP and suggested by Ellen Dannin for reforming the NLRA.[93]

Furthermore, Section 3 will also provide aggrieved employees a real choice as to whether they want to proceed with their union attorney or with a private attorney. This choice will promote union responsiveness and sensitivity to their members' needs. If the employee chooses the union attorney, then unions would recover the statutory fees at management attorney rates, which are typically significantly higher than union-side attorney rates.[94] The Seventh Circuit has described the "bargain rates" that union-side attorneys provide as a form of charity based on idealism.[95] "Some lawyers dedicate their professional lives to causes they find admirable and worthy of support—to legal services for the poor, to the representation of unions. These lawyers are making contributions to their favored causes, not in money but in time."[96]

The union's ability to have much of their litigation subsidized through statutory fees will allow unions to charge lower dues, and therefore allow members to retain more of their wages. Lastly, employers hate subsidizing unions, especially those employers that openly violate employees' rights in order to keep the union out. The payment of attorneys' fees for successful litigants would force employers to realize that unlawful labor practices are both economically and ideologically detrimental to their businesses.

Section 5 of the model statute allows individuals who are discriminated on the basis of seeking union membership to recover compensatory and punitive damages. The availability of compensatory damages acknowledges that an employee who suffers future pecuniary and non-pecuniary losses as a result of discriminatory conduct based on her union support suffers no less than if that conduct were based on an unlawful classification. The ability to collect punitive damages serves as a special deterrent to employers who choose to willfully violate the employee's rights.

Section 6 of the model statute acknowledges the NLRB's deep experience with labor law, while integrating the more successful process under Title VII. The details of labor law have been examined and developed incrementally by the adjudication arm of the NLRB for three-quarters of a century, and it would present a waste to abandon that deep reserve of knowledge and experience. The EEOC and NLRB follow the same regulations, so an aggrieved individual would not be prejudiced by being required to exhaust the process through one agency rather than the other.

Under an amended Civil Rights Act, an aggrieved employee alleging violations of her right to organize would still proceed by filing a charge with the NLRB. However, the NLRB would essentially be a stand-in for the EEOC. The NLRB would investigate the charge, as it currently does. If the investigation revealed that there is sufficient evidence of a violation of law, it would issue a notice of right-to-sue, just as the EEOC currently does. The aggrieved party would then have the option of proceeding through the NLRB process, involving a hearing before an ALJ, and the possibility of a board appeal, and court of appeals enforcement; or she would have the option of proceeding privately and bringing suit directly in federal court. Similarly if the NLRB investigation concluded that there was no violation of law, or if 180 days passed and the plaintiff requested, the NLRB would issue a notice of right-to-sue.

If the employee chose to pursue a private route, then all the provisions of the Civil Rights Act that make such private action feasible would be available to her, including those that allow an aggrieved party to afford an attorney (that is, attorneys' fees), gain relevant information during the pre-trial process and promote settlement prior to trial (that is, discovery), succeed at trial (that is, jury trials), and provide an incentive for an aggrieved party to pursue a suit (that is, back pay and the possibility of being awarded compensatory and punitive damages). Some employees may still choose to proceed under the current public NLRB approach, especially under the following circumstances: (1) where she is not able or willing to engage an attorney, and would prefer the government prosecute her charge; or (2) where she prefers the expedited procedures of an ALJ hearing. In instances where the employer's conduct is egregious, but the employee chooses to take no action, Section 7 allows the secretary of labor to proceed against the employer.

Section 8 of the model statute creates the bridge between the theoretical reconceptualization of labor rights as civil rights and a collective bargaining agreement. The amendments proposed here to the Civil Rights Act are basic—they only acknowledge that it is a civil right to be able to join or organize a labor organization. Once this organization is formed, it is still up to the union and employer to negotiate a collective bargaining agreement, and then operate according to the terms of that agreement. This will be especially tough if the employer is so intransigent that it is willing to violate the employees' civil rights in order to keep the union out. Therefore, Section 8 allows an employer that has already violated the employees' civil rights to limit its liability by entering into a collective bargaining agreement with an employee representative or a union, or if the employer begins negotiations with the union and agrees to submit to binding arbitration the terms of the contract should the parties fail to reach an agreement.

This provision does not encroach on the remedial purpose of the Civil Rights Act of making the individual whole, as it does not limit the back pay or compensatory damages. This provision follows the logic of Title VII, which limits an employer's liability if it offers to reinstate a fired employee unconditionally.[97] A similar provision that limited the employer's *overall* liability for signing a collective bargaining agreement would pit the individual employee who took risks to organize or join a union against the prospective union. Section 8 also follows the logic of the role of punitive damages in the law. The purpose of punitive damages is to punish those that have willfully violated the rights of others, in an attempt to curb such behavior in the future. The focus of punitive damages is always on the defendant rather than the plaintiff. Therefore, it makes immanent sense to limit this area of damages if the employer reverses its opposition to employees exercising their right to organize. In this instance, if an employer enters into a collective bargaining agreement after violating an employee's civil rights, this act accomplishes the general purpose of punitive damages.

An Amended Civil Rights Act, in Practice

An amended Civil Rights Act that included the right to join or not join a union would have a variety of practical effects. First and foremost, it would alter the scope of coverage of labor law to the more reasonable scope of the Civil Rights Act. Currently, federal labor law excludes from coverage agricultural laborers, supervisors, public sector employees, and independent contractors.[98] Many of the NLRA exclusions are historical artifacts, based on assumptions that have proven false, or stem from racism. Rather than address each of the problematic exclusions individually through the legislative process, as has been tried with some of these excluded groups,[99] this amendment to the Civil Rights Act would cover all these individuals at once, because the Civil Rights Act protects the individual rather than the statutory "employee."[100] Conceived as an individual right, there is no good reason to exclude these categories of individuals from coverage of federal labor law.

Agricultural Laborers

The NLRA excludes from coverage "agricultural laborers" in its definition section, meaning that all farmworker labor protections stem from state law.[101] The original reasons for this exclusion are not entirely known, as there is almost no discussion of this major exclusion in the legislative history of the act. Some have located the reason for the exclusion in Congress's desire not to interpose federal law in an area that was, at the time, largely non-industrialized and was run by families.[102] This explanation fits well with the NLRA's general focus on industry and manufacturing, often at the exclusion of other areas of employment. Others have located the reason for the exclusion as a form of racism that was part of much of the New Deal legislation.[103] Another piece of legislation that was intended to help those worst off and was signed within a month of the NLRA—the Social Security Act—also excluded agricultural laborers.[101] In 1935, a disproportionate number of agricultural laborers were

African-Americans in southern states, and southern senators sought to exclude "blacks by proxy" from coverage under the NLRA.[105]

Whatever the reasons for the exclusion of agricultural laborers, the effect of the exclusion is in stark contradiction to the express purpose of the NLRA. Agriculture in America today is largely industrial, and whatever the original reasons for this exclusion, there remains no strong policy rationale for the continued wholesale exclusion of agricultural laborers from the protections of labor law.

There are currently approximately 1.8 million full-time farmworkers in America,[106] and even though OSHA has stated that, "agriculture is the most hazardous industry in the nation,"[107] most of these farmworkers have few protections. Some of these farmworkers have been organized by the United Farm Workers of America (UFW) and other agricultural unions through risky organizing efforts that proceeded without federal protections, and have succeeded in gaining state-level protections. But one report noted many farmworkers "are exposed to harsh elements, working long hours in the sun, rain, and at times, cold. Their repetitive work includes stooping, twisting, operating heavy machinery, using sharp tools, climbing on ladders and carrying heavy loads. They are exposed to dust, dirt, fungi, plants, animals, insects and pesticides. Nearly every aspect of their work carries health risks ranging from cuts and sprains, to chronic life-endangering conditions."[108] Furthermore, the occupational fatality rate for farmworkers is more than six times higher than the national average occupational fatality rate, accounting for over 9,000 work-related fatalities from 1992 to 2009.[109]

In addition to the dangers of agriculture that are inherent in other highly physical labor occupations, agricultural laborers deal with a host of issues that would be mitigated greatly by collective action and concerted activity. According to the recent collaborative report from the United Farm Workers and the Bon Appétit Management Company, "Inventory of Farmworker Issues and Protections in the United States," among the issues about which farmworkers most often complain and for which they seek legal protection are: unpaid overtime and minimum wages, denial of rest and meal periods, retaliation and wrongful termination, sexual harassment, substandard housing, unsafe transportation of workers, and the like.[110]

A recent report by the Michigan Civil Rights Commission described in detail some of the substandard housing and working conditions that many migrant and seasonal farmworkers endure.[111] The report found that much of the housing that farmworkers were forced to live in because of their poverty and rural location of the worksites had structural defects, faulty wiring and gas leaks that led to explosions, overcrowding that led to the spread of communicable diseases, close proximity to pesticides, poor sanitation, rat and vermin infestations, and similar extreme living conditions.[112] With regard to the working conditions, the same report found that many workers did not have access to potable water or bathrooms in the fields, and were not afforded bathroom breaks even if such facilities were available.[113] In addition to the physically substandard conditions of their employment, many farmworkers must contend with outright wage theft by their employers.[114]

Despite the extreme hardships that these agricultural laborers face in the conditions of their employment, many farmworkers are explicitly exempted from even the most basic protections such as the minimum wage protections of the Fair Labor Standards Act (FLSA), and all of them are exempt from the overtime protections of the FLSA,[115] so they have no statutory remedy available for many wage violations.[116] Furthermore, though Title VII ostensibly protects farmworkers from conduct such as sexual harassment, many farmworkers are hesitant to assert their statutory rights because of poverty, isolation, fear of retaliation, and extreme dependency on their employers.[117]

An amended Civil Rights Act that protected agricultural laborers in their right to organize and bargain collectively would provide a framework through which these employees could mitigate many of these endemic concerns. Though the initial right to organize and join a union would be statutorily based, the union would serve as a strong platform for addressing health and safety concerns, wages, and other problems associated with the occupation or worksite. Unions would represent a form of self-help for farmworkers.

Supervisors

Supervisors have presented a unique area of confusion and controversy under the NLRA. Though they are currently excluded from coverage under the act, the explicit exclusion was not added to the NLRA until the Taft-Hartley amendments of 1947.[118] The Supreme Court case of *Packard Motor Car Co. v. NLRB*,[119] issued only several months before Taft-Hartley, and explicitly overruled by the act, captures well the tensions and controversies surrounding coverage of supervisors. In *Packard*, a group of foremen at the plant tried to organize and bargain collectively, but the company asserted that the foremen were not covered under the NLRA and refused to recognize the union.[120] In a 5-4 decision, the Supreme Court upheld the NLRB's holding that the foremen were protected by the NLRA. Justice William O. Douglas, however, wrote a strong dissent where he presented the inherent problems with allowing supervisors to organize in the post–World War II manufacturing economy. He argued that allowing supervisors to organize would "obliterate the line between management and labor."[121] Justice Douglas worried that if supervisors and every level of manager were permitted to organize, then "management and labor will become more of a solid phalanx than separate factions in warring camps."[122]

This statement expresses both the goals of the NLRA, and the problems inherent in supervisors organizing from the vantage point of the 1940s. The act recognizes an insurmountable conflict between employer and employee, and allows the government to intervene only to the point of creating a balance between the two, with the ultimate goal of promoting industrial peace and the free flow of commerce.[123] In the postwar industrial economy, any result that led to a breakdown of the barriers between employee and employer would necessarily be in conflict with the purpose of the act. Or, as the dissenting member of the NLRB framed the outcome of the board's holding that foremen could organize: it would take down all the "bars . . . which have hitherto been invoked to confine management and labor within their proper spheres of influence."[124]

The Taft-Hartley amendments adopted the dissent's view of employee and employer, and defined supervisors out of the act. In doing so, the act incorporated the company's view in *Packard* that "if foremen combine to bargain advantages for themselves, they will sometimes be governed by interests of their own or of their fellow foremen, rather than by the company's interest."[125] The legislative history of the supervisor exclusion also indicates that legislators felt that supervisors did not need the protections of federal labor legislation, as they already had a voice in the terms and conditions of their employment by virtue of their being supervisors.[126] Congress also expressed a fear that if supervisors unionized with other employees, the effect would be a company union that would manipulate the organization process.[127] The supervisor exclusion made sense in the 1940s, but today, this historically antiquated view of supervisors unfortunately remains fixed into federal labor law, despite the fact that the character of the American workforce has changed significantly since that time.

The NLRA defines supervisors using twelve job functions, in the disjunctive,[128] where performance of any one may be grounds for labeling an employee a supervisor,[129] so long as the authority requires the use of some "independent judgment," and is used "in the interest of the employer." This definition is quite broad and has proven difficult to apply to a wide variety of jobs, especially since the definition of "professional employees"—which are covered under the NLRA—has a large overlap with supervisory employees.[130] In 2006, the NLRB developed a three-pronged test to determine the nebulous definition of supervisor: the individual must be able to assign other employees with regard to their place, time, and duty; the individual must be accountable for the actions for those employees she assigns; and the individual must have discretion to make such assignments.[131] However, as the NLRB tried to locate the original intent of Taft-Hartley in creating this test, it lost sight of whether the nature of work and the workforce in America had so changed over the intervening sixty years that trying to recapture the act's intent may be at odds with the goals of the NLRA.[132] In analyzing the ways in which the modern economy is trending, some have observed that the supervisor exception may threaten to swallow the NLRA's general rule of coverage:

> It took six decades for the Board to enunciate a functional interpretation for Section 2(11), but that effort seems increasingly meaningless in a workplace where everyone will share some measure of supervisory duties. In such a world where everyone is a supervisor, will *anyone* have Section 7 rights under the Act? . . . Now it seems that in a self-directed twenty-first century workplace, *no one* may have a clear, undeniable right to join a union, free of challenge by employers.[133]

With this change in the nature of work in twenty-first-century America, the supervisor exclusion makes little sense.[134] Under the Civil Rights Act, supervisors are not excluded from coverage. Just as they receive the act's full protection against race, sex, or religious discrimination, they would receive protections against labor discrimination. The current NLRB rules concerning the makeup of the bargaining unit would still apply, meaning that supervisors would not be in the same bargaining unit as those employees that they supervise.

Public Employees

Public sector employees are not covered under the NLRA through the explicit exclusion in the definition of "employer": "The term 'employer'

. . . shall not include the United States or any wholly owned Government corporation, or any Federal Reserve Bank, or any State or political subdivision thereof."[135] The exclusion of public sector employees grew out of the early twentieth-century view that:

> It is generally conceded that association with an organization which, on any occasion or for any purpose, attempts to control the relations of members of either the police or fire departments toward the municipality they undertake to serve, is, in the very nature of things, inconsistent with the discipline which such employment imperatively requires, and therefore must prove subversive of the public service and detrimental to the general welfare.[136]

In other words, public sector unions were viewed with suspicion, with many fearing that public employees combining for the purpose of bettering their working conditions was inherently at odds with the public interest. Beyond the assertions of disloyalty, many held that public sector unions would be unlawful because they would be an unlawful delegation of power to private parties.[137] Furthermore, there was the belief that allowing public sector employees the right to organize would give these employees "special access to the political process."[138]

Many of the historical concerns against public sector unions have likewise proven largely unfounded, but this has not stopped recent reincarnations of these self-same arguments.[139] For many decades now, the federal government and a broad array of state and municipal governments have permitted public employees to form unions in order to bargain collectively. Most states already restrict the right to strike for certain types of employees, especially those whose work is essential to the health and safety of the public, such as police and firefighters. However, there has been no empirical evidence to suggest that there is a tension or incompatibility between public employment and organizing. Many public employees perform almost identical functions as their private counterparts—from professionals such as public school teachers and government attorneys to laborers that serve on work crews and as sanitary employees—and it makes little sense to permit one group to organize and exclude a similarly situated group based on false notions of public service. Accordingly, we believe the coverage of public employees under the Civil Rights Act is appropriate in a revised law that includes protection against discrimination for labor organizing.

The Right to Join or Not Join a Union

The current version of labor rights embodied in the NLRA and similar statutes is not conceived of as an individual right, but rather a collective right that flows to the individual through the union and is prosecuted by the government. In what has been termed "industrial pluralism," the workplace is seen as a mini-democracy, with the union and employer as legislators representing their constituencies' interests.[140] The goal under the industrial pluralist model was to create an equality of power between labor and management in order to achieve stability in the workplace.[141] As University of California Hastings law professor Reuel Schiller notes:

> Thus, according to the industrial pluralists, group action was a pre-requisite for industrial democracy. Only through collectivization could workers achieve the strength necessary to act as equal citizens in the industrial state. Pluralists viewed unions as interest groups, amassing the otherwise atomized power of workers. This emphasis on the necessity of the group caused industrial pluralists to discount the rights of individuals within those groups. As a Progressive during the Lochner era, [University of Wisconsin economist John R.] Commons viewed appeals to individual liberties with suspicion. This was the language of laissez-faire constitutionalism, used by state and federal courts to obstruct reform and, in the minds of Progressives like Commons, to entrench elites by denying the realities of bargaining power in industrialized America. Individual liberty was achieved through group strength. An individual in a union was "supreme but coerced," obtaining liberty through collectively negotiated rights under a bargaining agreement.[142]

The view of collective rights versus individual rights has shifted greatly since the passage of the NLRA in 1935. Individual rights, as exemplified by the Civil Rights Act, seek to protect the individual's dignity rather than an abstract promotion of a laissez-faire vision of the workplace. The Civil Rights Act protects individuals who have been treated unequally on the basis of their membership in a protected class in order to empower the individual and not reduce the individual to a stereotype of the class. Employment law that protects an individual's civil rights presents a different conception of the workplace than the industrial pluralists. It does not conceive of the workplace as having a pro-black or pro-female contingent consisting of employee members of those groups, and an anti-black or anti-female contingent consisting of management, that should have equal power and self-govern from that equality of strength. Such a model of civil rights would be bizarre, counter-productive, and against the foundations and basic rights upon which civil rights are built. The reorientation of labor rights as civil rights that stem from the First Amendment and belong to the individual means that all parts of those rights will be implicated, including the right to not join a union.

Under an amended civil rights regime, an individual must be protected in making either decision, whether to join a union or not join a union. Though it is unlikely that the latter instance of an employer coercing or disciplining an employee for not joining a union would occur to the same degree as an employer coercing or disciplining an employee for joining a union, the Civil Rights Act should fully protect both choices. This protection should follow the compromise followed by most states, wherein an employee may opt out of joining a union that has been designated the employee representative, but must still pay an "agency fee." Under this compromise, no employee must join a union that has been chosen as the sole bargaining representative, and therefore does not have to pay for union activities "beyond those germane to collective bargaining, contract administration, and grievance adjustment."[143] These "financial core payors" do not have to agree with, or financially support, the mission of the union, its outside political activities, or its stances on social issues, but they may not free-ride off the costly and beneficial work that the union performs with regards to the terms and conditions of employment.[144]

The "agency fee" has been described by the Supreme Court as an appropriate compromise between permitting the union to perform the necessary and costly work that it is intended to perform, while allowing individuals to opt out of compelled membership in an organization with which they may personally disagree. In *Abood v Detroit Board of Education* (1977), the Supreme Court declared:

> The designation of a union as exclusive representative carries with it great responsibilities. The tasks of negotiating and administering a collective-bargaining agreement and representing the interests of employees in settling disputes and processing grievances are continuing and difficult ones. They often entail expenditure of much time and money. The services of lawyers, expert negotiators, economists, and a research staff, as well as general administrative

personnel, may be required. Moreover, in carrying out these duties, the union is obliged "fairly and equitably to represent all employees . . . , union and nonunion," within the relevant unit. A union-shop arrangement has been thought to distribute fairly the cost of these activities among those who benefit, and it counteracts the incentive that employees might otherwise have to become "free riders" to refuse to contribute to the union while obtaining benefits of union representation that necessarily accrue to all employees.

To compel employees financially to support their collective-bargaining representative has an impact upon their First Amendment interests. An employee may very well have ideological objections to a wide variety of activities undertaken by the union in its role as exclusive representative. His moral or religious views about the desirability of abortion may not square with the union's policy in negotiating a medical benefits plan. One individual might disagree with a union policy of negotiating limits on the right to strike, believing that to be the road to serfdom for the working class, while another might have economic or political objections to unionism itself. An employee might object to the union's wage policy because it violates guidelines designed to limit inflation, or might object to the union's seeking a clause in the collective-bargaining agreement proscribing racial discrimination. The examples could be multiplied. To be required to help finance the union as a collective-bargaining agent might well be thought, therefore, to interfere in some way with an employee's freedom to associate for the advancement of ideas, or to refrain from doing so, as he sees fit. But the judgment clearly made in *Hanson* and *Street* is that such interference as exists is constitutionally justified by the legislative assessment of the important contribution of the union shop to the system of labor relations established by Congress.[145]

The alternative to the agency fee compromise described above are the so-called "right to work" laws allowed by the Taft-Hartley Act.[146] "Right to work" laws ban union security agreements, which require all employees in the bargaining unit to become members of the union or pay an agency fee, and allow employees covered under a union contract to choose whether they wish to pay union dues.[147] "Right to work" laws have been passed by twenty-three states, and they go so far in providing the individual the choice not to join a union, that they deprive the individual of the choice to join a union.[148] Studies have shown that "Right to work" laws have greatly diminished union density and wages among all workers because of the financial incentives for employees to choose not to pay union dues, while still receiving all the benefits of the union.[149] In an ostensible attempt to offer employees the choice to be free "from the tyranny of organized labor,"[150] "Right to work" laws result in a loss of choice for many workers in these states.

Under the amended Civil Rights Act proposed here, the right to join or not join a union is cast as an individual right and therefore must fully protect either choice that an employee may make. An employee choosing not to join the union has two opportunities to exercise this choice. First, she may simply vote against the union in an election or refuse to sign an authorization card. The union must receive support from 50 percent plus one of all voting employees in order to be recognized as the employees' representative.[151] If the union received majority support and an employee in the bargaining unit still wished not to join the union, she could forego full union membership and become a "financial core payor" whose payments would only be used for activities that were germane to collective bargaining, contract administration, and grievance adjustment. An employee who was discriminated on the basis of exercising her right not to join the union would have the full protections of the Civil Rights Act in the same way as an employee who was discriminated against for choosing to join the union.

Conclusion

For far too long, American law has been marked by an indefensible distinction between employment law, which has largely effective and adequate procedures and remedies and labor law, which has neither. It is time to collapse that dichotomy. In the next chapter, we examine the many reasons why the Civil Rights Act is a well-suited vehicle for labor law reform.

CHAPTER SIX

Why the Civil Rights Act Is the Right Vehicle to Protect Labor Organizing

Is it appropriate to use the Civil Rights Act—a sacred text in America's struggle for racial justice—to protect people who are trying to organize a union? Is joining a union a basic civil right, like the right not to be discriminated against based on immutable factors such as race or national origin? Does the fact that firing someone for joining a union is economically rational—it will hurt a company's bottom line—make it more justifiable than other types of discrimination?

In this chapter, we advance three main arguments for suggesting that the Civil Rights Act is the right vehicle for protecting union organizing. First, the freedom to join a union has been long recognized as a basic human right in U.S. and international law, and nondiscrimination laws have for many years protected individuals not only for who they are but for the actions they take. These rights remain intact whether or not they hurt a company's profitability. Second, strengthening labor can help advance the objectives of the original Civil Rights Act by promoting human dignity and equality, particularly for people of color. The civil rights and labor movements have a strongly shared set of values, interests, tactics, and adversaries, and more vibrant unions can promote these values and interests, helping to enhance the civil rights agenda. Third, stronger unions, by reducing employer discretion over personnel decisions, and by setting up grievance procedures for violations, will likely reduce instances of discrimination based on race, gender, national origin, or religion—reinforcing key goals of the original act.

Labor Organizing as a Basic Human Right

As we noted earlier, the freedom to join a union in order to advance one's interests and values has long been recognized as a basic human right. Section 7 of the National Labor Relations Act of 1935 (NLRA) recognizes the "right to self-organization, to form, join, or assist labor organizations, to bargain collectively through representatives of their own choosing, and to engage in concerted activities for the purpose of collective bargaining or other mutual aid and protection." The 1948 Universal Declaration of Human Rights, likewise, declares in Article 23 that "everyone has the right to form and to join trade unions for the protection of his interests."

The Right of Association

The right to organize is closely related to the United States Constitution's right to "freedom of association." In a democracy, the right of individuals to band together and pursue their interests with like-minded people is considered an essential element of freedom, and in the United States, this right has been especially well exercised. As Alexis de Tocqueville remarked, "In no other country in the world has the principle of association been more successfully used or applied toward a greater multitude of objects than in America."[1] Although the U.S. Constitution does not specifically mention "freedom of association," the U.S. Supreme Court long ago recognized that First Amendment free speech and freedom of assembly provisions necessarily imply a corollary right to freedom of association.

In the landmark 1958 case of *NAACP v. Alabama,* the Supreme Court held that the State of Alabama could not compel the NAACP to disclose its membership rolls, as doing so would produce a chilling effect on the right of individuals to join the NAACP and advocate for racial equality. The Court declared: "Effective advocacy of both public and private points of view, particularly controversial ones, is undeniably enhanced by group association, as this Court has more than once recognized by remarking upon the close nexus between the freedoms of speech and assembly."[2] This right to association was not limited to pursuing political activity, the Court found. "Of course, it is immaterial whether the beliefs sought to be advanced by association pertain to political, economic, religious or cultural matters, and state action which may have the effect of curtailing the freedom to associate is subject to the closest scrutiny."[3]

Moreover, the Supreme Court has specifically applied the right of association to labor unions, striking down government efforts to quash union-based associational rights. In *Thomas v. Collins* (1945), for example, the Court voided a Texas law that required union officials to register with the state before engaging in union organizing activities, suggesting that such a requirement interfered with the "rights of assembly and discussion" that "are protected by the First Amendment."[4] Likewise, in *Smith v. Arkansas State Highway Employees Local* (1979), the Court suggested in dicta that "the Constitution forbids" a highway commission from "prohibit[ing] its employees from joining together in a union, from persuading others to do so, or from advocating any particular ideas."[5]

The Constitution, of course, restrains government, not private employers. But the NLRA—and the Civil Rights Act—essentially extend constitutional rights (to be treated equally regardless of race and to freely associate) to private sector employees. Conceptually, considering labor organizing as a human right does not break new ground; rather it incorporates the right into a statute, the Civil Rights Act, which has stronger penalties than those provided under the NLRA.

Anti-Discrimination Laws Protect Volitional Acts, Not Just Immutable Characteristics

Some might object that the Civil Rights Act should be reserved for protection against discrimination based on characteristics that are immutable, such as race, ethnicity, or national origin, as opposed to discrimination based on choices that individuals make, such as trying to become part of a union. But the Civil Rights Act has long covered mutable traits that can involve individual choice, such as religious affiliation or pregnancy.[6] An individual who chooses to convert to a religion disfavored by her employer is protected by the Civil Rights Act, even though changing religions was an act of volition.

As noted in chapter 5, moreover, the list of protected categories has expanded over time to prohibit discrimination against a variety of mutable characteristics. The Uniformed Services Employment and Reemployment Rights Act (USERRA), for example, bars discrimination against individuals who choose to serve in the armed forces. The law provides, "A person who is a member of, applies to be a member of, performs, has performed, applies to perform, or has an obligation to perform service in a uniformed service shall not be denied initial employment, reemployment, retention in employment, promotion, or any benefit of employment by an employer on the basis of that membership, application for membership, performance of service, application for service, or obligation."[7] The U.S. bankruptcy code, likewise, prohibits discrimination in employment for those who have filed for bankruptcy. The law states, "No private employer may terminate the employment of, or discriminate with respect to employment against, an individual who is or has been a debtor under this title, a debtor or bankrupt under the Bankruptcy Act, or an individual associated with such debtor or bankrupt."[8]

Under the Occupational Safety and Health Act, individuals who choose to report unsafe and unhealthy conditions, environmental problems, and certain public hazards are protected against discrimination. As the U.S. Department of Labor notes, "Whistleblowers may not be transferred, denied a raise, have their hours reduced, or be fired or punished in any other way because they have exercised any right afforded to them under one of the laws that protect whistleblowers."[9]

A number of states, including Hawaii, Minnesota, New Mexico, Connecticut, and Massachusetts prohibit automatic discrimination against applicants for employment who have been convicted of a crime. These "ban the box" laws forbid employers from asking "if a job applicant had a conviction on his record until after they had decided if the person was qualified for the job."[10] The District of Columbia's Human Rights Act bars discrimination not only based on such factors as race and color, but also marital status, family responsibilities, matriculation, political affiliation, source of income, or place of residence or business.[11] Finally, in 2011, President Barack Obama backed legislation to ban discrimination against individuals who have been unemployed, citing examples of job postings which would only consider applicants who are currently employed.[12]

In sum, civil rights protections have never been limited to immutable characteristics; and the list of protected categories has not been static or frozen so as to protect only those criteria that were part of the original 1964 act. Civil rights groups generally recognize that enlarging the circle of groups and actions protected by civil rights statutes is a positive development that has in no way diminished the core rights of women and people of color. In 2004, for example, Julian Bond, then chairman of the NAACP, suggested that the gay rights movement does not in any way detract from the civil rights movement for African Americans. He declared, "We ought to be flattered that our movement has provided so much inspiration for others, that it has been so widely imitated, and that our tactics, methods, heroines and heroes, even our songs, have been appropriated by or served as models for others." He continued, "The right not to be discriminated against is a commonplace claim we all expect to enjoy under our laws and our founding document, the Constitution. That many had to struggle to gain these rights makes them precious—it does not make them special and it does not reserve them only for me or restrict them from others."[13]

Corporate Profits Do Not Trump Civil Rights

Likewise, the fact that discrimination might be economically rational because it boosts a firm's profits is not a justification in American law. The NLRA prohibits discriminating against employees trying to organize a union, whether or not such actions hurt employer profitability. And the Civil Right Act has required nondiscriminatory policies even where they might reduce corporate profits. In the 1971 case of *Diaz v. Pan American World Airlines,* for example, the Fifth Circuit ruled that even though research found that airplane passengers overwhelmingly preferred female flight attendants (and might therefore be more likely to fly on an airplane that discriminated against male flight attendant applicants), Pan Am could not use this evidence to justify sex discrimination.[14] So too, in the 1981 case of *Wilson v. Southwest Airlines,* a district court, citing *Diaz,* noted, "If an employer could justify employment discrimination merely on the grounds that it is necessary to make a profit, Title VII would be nullified in short order."[15]

Strengthening Labor Advances the Larger Goals of the Civil Rights Act

If including the basic right to organize as part of the Civil Rights Act makes sense on its own merits, the close connection between the civil rights and labor movements further strengthens the rationale. Although organized labor has, like many American institutions, been unforgivably marred by a history of racism, many have recognized that the civil rights and labor movements share basic values, interests, tactics, and adversaries, all of which makes the Civil Rights Act a fitting vehicle for advancing labor rights.

There can be no whitewashing of the history of racial and gender discrimination in the trade union movement. For many years, labor unions were not immune from the vicious racism and sexism that was a part of virtually all American institutions, including religious and governmental entities. Some unions officially barred black workers from joining. For years, A. Philip Randolph, the African American head of the Brotherhood of Sleeping Car Porters, offered resolutions calling on the AFL-CIO to expel segregated unions, prompting an irate George Meany, president of the AFL-CIO, to lash out at Randolph at a 1959 meeting, declaring, "Who the hell appointed you as the guardian of all the Negroes in America?"[16] As late as 1961, Martin Luther King Jr. chastised the AFL-CIO for continuing to include unions that barred blacks from membership.[17] In 1963, under Meany's leadership, the AFL-CIO refused to endorse the March on Washington, even as many individual unions did actively participate.

Even with all those stains of racism, however, King, Randolph, and Bayard Rustin, the organizer of the March on Washington, each argued that labor was an indispensable ally to the civil rights movement in the fight for social justice. At the 1961 AFL-CIO convention, King declared, "The two most dynamic and cohesive liberal forces in the country are the labor movement and the Negro freedom movement. Together we can be architects of democracy."[18] Rustin, likewise, argued in 1965, "The labor movement, despite its obvious faults, has been the largest single organized force in this country pushing for progressive social legislation."[19]

Shared Values

Fundamentally, the labor movement and the civil rights movement are both concerned about the same principles: the dignity of individuals, who have the right to be respected and valued whatever their job or race; the importance of equality, both racial and economic; the centrality of the right to vote—both for elected representatives in government and for union leadership—to bring about greater political and workplace democracy; and the salience of human solidarity, the need to rise above our atomized existence to join together to improve the larger society. These common values led Randolph to head both the Brotherhood of Sleeping Car Porters union, and to threaten the original March on Washington in 1941, which prompted President Franklin D. Roosevelt to ban discrimination in the defense industries.[20] Shared values led Rustin to head the A. Philip Randolph Institute, where he built bridges between labor and the civil rights movement. Mutual principles led King to embrace the Montgomery Bus Boycott and the Selma voting rights march for racial justice on the one hand, and the Memphis sanitation workers strike and the Poor People's Campaign for economic justice on the other. And these common values led all three men to spearhead the legendary 1963 March on Washington, with Randolph as chairman, Rustin as chief organizer, and King as the march's most celebrated speaker. The march merged the goals of both movements—it was a March for Jobs and Freedom—and though it is mostly remembered as a landmark in the fight for civil rights, it originated as a labor march.[21]

Animated by shared values, the two movements aided one another. In the 1950s, unions, such as the United Auto Workers, supported the Montgomery Bus Boycott, and King's Southern Christian Leadership Conference received 80 percent of its first year funding from the United Packinghouse Workers Unions of America.[22] In the 1960s, the AFL-CIO provided critical political support to help pass the Civil Rights and Voting Rights Acts, with some suggesting that the former "never would have passed" without labor.[23] The labor-civil rights coalition, writes historian Michael K. Honey, together "ultimately broke the back of Jim Crow."[24]

The civil rights movement, meanwhile, supported labor. As King noted, "If the Negro wins, labor wins." Emancipated and energized black voters in Louisiana, he noted in his 1961 speech to the AFL-CIO, helped repeal an anti-union "right to work" law.[25] To formalize the partnership, Randolph worked with labor and civil rights groups and others to form an umbrella organization, the Leadership Conference on Civil and Human Rights, in 1950.[26]

Shared Interests, Shared Enemies

The alliance between the civil rights and labor movements was born not only of similar values but also what King called "the kinship of interests."[27] Unions have a powerful interest in reducing racial discrimination and animus because racial hostility inhibits worker solidarity and union organizing, a fact well known to employers who historically sought to divide and conquer workers of different races.[28] Black people, meanwhile, have an interest in helping organized labor because blacks are disproportionately a working people, they get an even larger wage premium than whites when they join unions, and traditionally they have desired to join unions at higher rates than whites. Meanwhile, both elements of the coalition—labor and civil rights—need one another as allies in the larger fight for social justice.

Racial animus has always been a key impediment to union organizing, which helps explain why the American South has historically been most resistant to unions. In the 1940s, the CIO launched "Operation Dixie" to organize the South, and part of its agenda included efforts to reduce discrimination. As historian Tami Friedman notes, the CIO, with a $1 million war chest and 250 organizers, set out in 1946 to organize at least 1 million workers by the end of the year. The AFL also made a pledge to organize 1 million Southern workers. The threat to Southern segregationists was clear as the CIO president Philip Murray promised both "political and economic emancipation" for southern workers, and vowed to defeat two major segregationists in Mississippi.[29] W.E.B. Du Bois called the CIO the best hope for equal rights in the post-World War II era.[30]

With President Truman also beginning to move forward on civil rights, Southern segregationists ramped up their anti-union efforts. As the CIO began Operation Dixie, Southern Democrats joined Northern Republicans in voting for the Taft-Hartley legislation to cripple union organizing. Friedman writes,

> While the measure is often seen as the work of a Republican-dominated Congress, southern Democrats were instrumental in its passage; in both houses, over 80 percent of southern Democrats backed the bill. After President Truman vetoed the legislation, 90 percent of southern Democrats in the House of Representatives and over 77 percent of those in the Senate helped override his action.[31]

Southern conservatives feared that if unions united working-class whites and blacks, it could upend the politics of the South, where Jim Crow laws helped keep white and black workers on opposite sides of the political fence. White southerners pushed the argument that unions could bring "black domination in the South."[32] For King, the unity of interests of labor and civil rights groups was underlined by segregationist opposition to both. He noted, "the forces that are anti-Negro are by and large anti-labor."[33] He told the AFL-CIO in 1961 "the labor-hater and labor-baiter is virtually always a twin-headed creature spewing anti-Negro epithets from one mouth and anti-labor propaganda from the other mouth."[34]

Southern segregationists followed up their support for Taft-Hartley with an array of state-based "right to work" laws, which weaken unions by allowing employees to be "free riders"—benefiting from union collective bargaining but not contributing dues. To this day, the states most resistant to unions are those in the former Confederacy and the Jim Crow South. Of the seventeen states that had legally required segregation prior to *Brown v. Board of Education,* twelve are today "right to work" states.[35] All five states that ban collective bargaining with public employees—Georgia, North Carolina, South Carolina, Texas, and Virginia—are from the Jim Crow South.[36] And, according to the Bureau of Labor Statistics, the eleven states with the lowest rates of unionization are North Carolina, Arkansas, Georgia, Louisiana, Mississippi, South Carolina, Virginia, Tennessee, Texas, Oklahoma, and Florida. All of these states were formerly segregated.[37]

Meanwhile, just as labor has an interest in reducing racial animus to promote organizing, black Americans have always had an interest in promoting a stronger labor movement. As King noted, "Negroes are almost entirely a working people," far more likely to be employees than employers.[38] While unions for many years did practice racial discrimination, the stereotype of the typical union member as an aging white male blue-collar worker today is outdated. According to the Bureau of Labor Statistics, in 2010, 63 percent of union members were female, African American, and/or Latino.[39]

Blacks also benefit disproportionately from joining a union. In 2006, according to the Leadership Conference on Civil and Human Rights, the umbrella group for labor, civil rights and religious groups, the wage premium was 30 percent for the typical union worker, but 36 percent for unionized African Americans compared with their nonunion counterparts, and 46 percent for unionized Hispanic workers compared with nonunionized Hispanics. The Leadership Conference noted: "Even after taking into account factors that affect wages (experience, education, region, industry, occupation and marital status), union wage premiums for women and people of color remain sizable—10.5 percent for women, 20.3 percent for African Americans, 21.9 percent for Hispanics and 16.7 percent for Asian Americans." Minority and female workers appear to have a higher wage premium in part because unions negotiate uniform wages and benefits (reducing chances for discrimination) and because women and minorities are over-represented in low wage fields, where the union premium tends to be higher.[40]

Not surprisingly, African Americans are substantially more likely to desire to join a union—and are therefore especially hurt by current laws that impose weak penalties on firms that engage in unfair labor practices. According to Harvard University economist Richard B. Freeman and Joel Rogers of the University of Wisconsin, 59 percent of black workers (compared with 28 percent of non-black workers) support organizing their workplace. Women are also more likely than men to support organizing (35 percent to 27 percent).[41]

Finally, both the labor and civil rights movements know that a part-nership makes them each stronger than they would be individually. As Bayard Rustin argued in his famous article, "From Protest to Politics": "Neither [the labor] movement nor the country's twenty million black people can win political power alone. We need allies."[42]

Shared Tactics

Bound by common values, interests, and enemies, the labor movement and the civil rights movement also share common tactics. As King noted in his 1961 address to the AFL-CIO, the civil rights movement learned from the labor movement that it cannot rely on the charity of those in charge, and that power had to be seized because, as Victor Hugo noted, "there was always more misery in the lower classes than there was humanity in the upper classes." King told the audience: "Negroes in the United States read the history of labor and find it mirrors their own experience."[43] He drew parallels between the 1936 sit-down strike of autoworkers and the 1960s lunch counter sit-ins of black youth. In a 1961 speech to the United Auto Workers, King said that in the 1930s, "you creatively stood up for your rights by sitting down at your machines, just as our courageous students are sitting down at lunch counters across the South." The civil rights movement's use of "sit-ins, civil disobedience and protests" mimicked the labor movement's use of "strikes," and "demonstrations."[44]

Interestingly, Southern segregationists also used the same tactic against civil rights supporters as firms use today against workers trying to join a union: economic intimidation. In the 1950s, a number of Southern states passed legislation banning teachers from being members of "subversive" organizations, including the NAACP, forcing teachers to choose between resigning their NAACP membership or losing their jobs.[45] Likewise, employers who were part of the White Citizens' Councils in Southern states used economic pressure and intimidation to coerce blacks to with-draw from petitions supportive of racial integration.[46] Civil rights groups see echoes from the Jim Crow past in today's efforts by corporations to fire employees for exercising their rights to join a union.

Labor Enhances Protections of Civil Rights Act

Finally, it is fitting to include protections for labor organizing under the Civil Rights Act because the existence of a union in a workplace can, for a variety of reasons, discourage discrimination based on factors such as race and gender. In this way, adding labor organizing can advance the original underlying goals of the act itself.

Unions Decrease Employer Discretion to Discriminate

For one thing, unions decrease the discretion of employers to make arbitrary and abusive decisions to fire workers or to pay some workers more than others—which can reduce the opportunity for discrimination. Many Americans do not realize that most employees work "at will," meaning they can be fired for any reason or no reason at all. Unions, by contrast, usually bargain for the right to be fired only for "just cause." This higher standard for termination helps minority or female employees who are discriminated against because it is much easier to prove that a termination was unjust or arbitrary rather than having to go further and prove that it was also motivated by race or sex discrimination.

Likewise, because unions tend to bargain for uniform wages, they reduce employer discretion to pay minority and female employees less than white and male employees. Researchers find that the greater use of "objective pay setting criteria such as job classification and tenure" helps explain why the wage differentials between men and women and blacks and whites tend to be lower in unionized firms than nonunionized firms.[47] As the Leadership Conference on Civil Rights notes, "Collective bargaining agreements set terms and conditions of employment in unionized workplaces, making employment practices more transparent and, hence, less likely to be arbitrary and discriminatory."[48]

Sometimes, negotiated contracts provide bans on discrimination, which can, says the Leadership Conference, add "another layer of protection" for employees.[49] Unions also educate workers about their rights, so union members are more likely to recognize when wrongdoing and discrimination has occurred. Because unions provide a counterbalance to management's authority, the mere presence of the union can often deter abusive employer practices, including discrimination.

Union Procedures and Support

In addition to reducing management's discretion to discriminate, and leveling the playing field, unions usually bargain for contracts that put into place procedures to address grievances—including those having to do with race or sex discrimination—that can address problems more efficiently and cheaply than can litigation. As Julius Getman of the University of Texas notes, the grievance process established under collective bargaining agreements usually provides that "employer decisions may be challenged before a neutral third-party arbitrator with broad powers to review and set aside."[50] These grievance procedures provide an important supplement to civil rights protections. The Leadership Conference notes: "While not a substitute for the right to go to court, access to the grievance process is important to women and people of color, because it is less expensive, time-consuming and contentious than litigation; it engages the union directly in representing aggrieved workers; and it promotes faster resolution of disputes."[51] Research by Ann Hodges of the University of Richmond found that on the question of sexual harassment, union grievance procedures are "generally quicker and less expensive than litigation" yet still provide access to "a neutral arbitrator."[52]

Moreover, in instances where employees do wish to bring discrimination suits all the way to federal court, unions can provide legal counsel to discrimination victims and also provide them with financial benefits to help compensate for wages lost during a suit. Says the Leadership Conference: "The added heft unions bring in challenging discrimination is critical: fair employment laws ban a panoply of practices that have the intention or effect of discriminating, but equal opportunity is not a self-enforcing promise."[53]

Unions offer other protections against discrimination. In cases of sexual harassment, for example, mangers often retaliate against employees who dare to complain, which can effectively intimidate victims. Hodges found that unions often protect against such retaliation. Likewise, because unions represent all members, they can build up institutional memory of discrimination and identify larger patterns by employers that an individual victim might miss.[54]

The protections that unions provide against discrimination are especially important in low-wage jobs, where employers are both more likely to act arbitrarily and where women and employees of color are more likely to be concentrated.[55] Overall, researchers find that plaintiffs in unionized firms are more likely to be successful with their employment discrimination suits; and they are "less likely to be dismissed or to settle early."[56] In total, scholars conclude that, for a variety of reasons—including more uniform pay scales and the availability of grievance procedures—there appears to be "less discrimination among union workers."[57]

Conclusion

Protecting union organizing as a part of the Civil Rights Act, in sum, can be justified on its own merits, as the right to organize is important in a democratic society. But the evidence in this chapter suggests that the case is even stronger. Broadly speaking, the labor and civil rights movements share similar values and interests. And unions can help reduce discrimination in the workforce. In these senses, adding labor organizing to the Civil Rights Act helps further the agenda of the civil rights movement.

It is telling that, toward the end of his life, King put "justice for poor and working class people at the center of his agenda," as historian Michael Honey notes.[58] In launching the Poor People's campaign to address economic issues across racial lines, King declared, we are going to "enlarge this campaign into something bigger than just a civil rights movement for Negroes."[59] He began speaking of "two Americas," not as black and white, but rich and poor.[60] And for King, says Honey, unions were "the first anti-poverty program."[61]

Symbolic in King's shift in emphasis was his decision to aid striking sanitation workers in what would turn out to be the last days of his life. "In going to Memphis," Honey writes, "King returned to an issue he had fought for all of his life: the right of working people to organize unions of their own choosing."[62] The economic justice agenda can, in many ways, be seen as King's way of rounding out the original campaign for civil rights. Speaking to AFSCME workers in Memphis on March 18, 1968, King declared, "What does it profit a man to be able to eat at an integrated lunch counter if he doesn't earn enough money to buy a hamburger and a cup of coffee?"[63]

CHAPTER SEVEN

The Political Advantages of the Civil Rights Approach over Labor Law Reform

Given how exceedingly difficult it has proven to be to enact labor law reform over the past half century, what are the political prospects of amending the Civil Rights Act to protect those trying to organize a union? Business interests and most Republicans are likely to oppose any effort that improves the lot of unions, whatever label is placed on the reform. But when progressives next capture both houses of Congress and the executive branch, does a civil rights approach offer a greater likelihood of passage than traditional labor law reform? We think the evidence suggests it does, because the concept of "rights"—particularly "civil rights"—is deeply appealing to the American public. Framing labor organizing as a civil right moves the discussion from a struggle over raw interests to the higher realm of deeply held moral values.

In this chapter, we begin by reviewing the earlier failed efforts to reform labor law, under Presidents Lyndon Johnson, Jimmy Carter, Bill Clinton, and Barack Obama. The evidence suggests that reform failed each time, despite Democratic majorities in both houses of Congress, in part because labor law is complex, and opponents could exploit that complexity to distort the debate. Likewise, it appears that the issue was viewed by many, including many Democrats, as one of interests, not values, and turned on labor's raw strength, not its message.

We go on to explain the potential political advantages of applying a civil rights lens to labor law reform: the focus on discrimination against those engaged in labor organizing is a simple and straightforward question, which isolates the egregious behavior of employers from other questions raised by comprehensive labor law reform; the connection to helping expand the civil rights movement may very well energize progressives in a way that labor law reform does not; and the "rights" frame taps into deeply held individualistic American values in a way that labor's traditional emphasis on group solidarity does not. These three advantages—coupled with a larger public mood that is skeptical of corporations and angry about rising inequality—suggest that amending the Civil Rights Act could be more successful than past efforts to amend labor law.

The Failure of Labor Law Reform (1965–2009)

Four times between 1965 and 2009, Democrats held the White House and majorities in the Senate and House, and four times, efforts to remedy inequities in American labor law failed to prevail. The first attempt came under President Lyndon Johnson, when Democrats, on the heels of the 1964 landslide, sought to repeal section 14(b) of the Taft-Hartley Act, giving states the ability to adopt anti-labor "right to work" laws. The legislation passed the House of Representatives by a vote of 221 to 203, but in 1966 secured only 51 votes in the Senate (with 48 against), far short of the necessary supermajority to break a filibuster.[1]

In 1977, when Jimmy Carter was president, labor law reform legislation was introduced to stiffen penalties for employers who broke the law by firing workers engaged in organizing; expedite hearings; and deny federal contracts to repeat violators. The legislation passed the House by an overwhelming 252 to 163 margin. With Democrats holding 61 seats in the Senate, one opponent of the legislation later recalled, there "didn't seem any way to stop it." At President Carter's urging, however, the Senate squandered momentum on a fight over the Panama Canal Treaty. After an eventual five-week fight over labor law reform in 1978, the bill died in the Senate by a vote of 58 to 39, just two short of cloture to end a filibuster.[2]

Organized labor came back in 1993, under President Bill Clinton, with the Workplace Fairness Act, which sought to outlaw the permanent replacement of strikers. Once again, the legislation easily passed the House of Representatives on a vote of 239 to 190, but was stopped in a Democratic Senate, with a vote of 53 to 46, short of the necessary supermajority needed to break a filibuster.[3]

Finally, in 2009, under President Barack Obama, supporters of the Employee Free Choice Act (EFCA) thought they had a chance to pass important labor law reform, given Democratic control of both houses of Congress and the executive branch. EFCA, also known as "card check," would have allowed employees to certify a bargaining representative if a majority of workers signed on, voiding the need for a secret-ballot election. It also would have enhanced penalties for employers who engaged in unfair labor practices, such as wrongfully discharging employees trying to organize a union. And the legislation set forth procedures for reaching an initial collective bargaining agreement—if necessary, through arbitration—once a union was certified or recognized.[4]

The bill had strong support in the House of Representatives, where, two years earlier, in a March 2007 test vote, EFCA had passed by a margin of 241 to 185.[5] In 2009, Democrats had an even larger House majority than in 2007. And in the Senate, for a time, Democrats and those caucusing with them had a 60-vote filibuster-proof majority, giving labor some hope that a compromise version of EFCA could pass. But the defection of a Southern Democratic senator in April 2009 was a serious blow; and the death of Massachusetts senator Edward M. Kennedy and surprise election of a Republican, Scott Brown, to replace him in January 2010 brought hopes of passage to an end without a formal vote in either the Senate or the House.[6] EFCA, write political scientists Jacob Hacker and Paul Pierson, was "one of the few initiatives that might have had broader political significance by shifting the balance of organized power in Washington," but it "never got started."[7]

Why Labor Law Reform Has Failed

First and foremost, fierce and unified business opposition to labor law reform helps explain why each of the four efforts at reform went down in defeat. But labor reform was frustrated for two additional reasons over which labor has greater control for the future. First, labor law reform was seen as a highly complicated matter, which gave opponents an opening to distort labor's intentions. Second, reform was seen as a special interest fight between labor and business, which did not capture the imagination of the public or other progressive groups. As a result, organized labor had to rely on its own power, which is unevenly dispersed across the country, leaving it vulnerable in states with low rates of union density.

Labor law reform presents a number of technical legal issues that are poorly understood by the general public. The public has minimal understanding of the federal court system, but even less of the complicated set of rules administered by the National Labor Relations Board (NLRB). The most recent iteration of labor law reform, the Employee Free Choice Act, was described by a Gallup pollster as "a complex piece of legislation with numerous components." Perhaps because of its complexity, Gallup found in a 2009 poll that only 12 percent of Americans followed the issue "very closely," a level that Gallup described as "exceptionally low relative to public attention to other news issues Gallup has measured over the last two decades."[8]

The complexity of labor law reform efforts such as EFCA, in turn, made them vulnerable to mischaracterization by opponents, just as the complex nature of health care reform gave an opening to opponents to fuel rumors about "death panels" or coverage for illegal immigrants. In particular, the inclusion of card check provisions gave business opposition a chance to characterize EFCA as an effort to "end the right of employees to secret ballot elections."[9] Rather than having to defend employer behavior, including the termination of employees for trying to join a union, business changed the discussion to collective bargaining elections, and promoted stereotypes of union thugs ready to intimidate workers into signing cards certifying a union.

In addition, over the years, labor law reform has been seen largely as a special interest battle between labor and business and has not galvanized a broad coalition of progressives to come to labor's aid in pushing reform. Labor lawyer Thomas Geoghegan notes, "You meet other activists, go to their meetings. They understand each other's causes but have no sense of yours."[10] Many see labor as a "historical" movement, something from the past that is no longer central to today's fights. As a result, in political battles over its own future, labor has been largely on its own.[11]

In a detailed analysis of the 1978 Senate vote on labor law reform, for example, Harvard University economist Richard Freeman found that it was not political party membership but a state's union density that best predicted support or opposition to reform. Out of the twenty senators from the ten states with the lowest unionization rates (bottom quintile), only one voted in favor of the bill; and out of the twenty senators from the next lowest quintile, only six voted in favor of the legislation. Meanwhile, Senators from the ten states with the highest unionization rates (top quintile) voted 18 to 2 in favor of the bill; and Senators from the next highest quintile voted 17 to 3 in favor of the legislation.[12] Democratic Senator Dale Bumpers of Arkansas, a low union-density state, cast a decisive vote in killing the 1978 reform. And in a cruel repeat of history, in 2009, Senator Blanche Lincoln (D-AR), came out in opposition to the Employee Free Choice Act, dealing the bill a devastating setback.[13]

The fact that labor law reform is not seen as a basic litmus test issue for Democrats—and that other progressives have not adequately rallied behind unions in their hours of need—means that labor stands alone, and reform rises or falls on labor's own strength or weakness. As a result, the current approach to labor law reform puts unions in a political catch-22: organized labor cannot get reform of labor laws until it has greater political clout; but it cannot grow stronger and gain clout until it achieves labor law reform.

The Civil Rights Paradigm as a Way Out?

The discouraging history of efforts to reform the National Labor Relations Act (NLRA) over the past forty-five years is yet another reason to consider the civil rights approach. Whereas labor law reform is complicated and allows employers to focus public attention on union behavior, the civil rights approach is straightforward and puts focus directly on employer abuses of individual rights. Whereas labor law reform is seen as a battle between interests, and does not excite many progressives, civil rights discussions raise basic principles about nondiscrimination in the workplace that may bring labor more political allies. Whereas labor law reform naturally appeals to the concept of solidarity, regrettably an uphill battle in American culture, the focus on a "right" to unionize conforms better to the individualistic ethos at the heart of the American belief system. Finally, the advantages of the new civil rights approach could be applied at a time when the public appears more serious than ever about addressing root issues of economic inequality and the declining middle class.

A Simple Message Focusing on Employer Behavior

Unlike more comprehensive and complex reforms of labor law, amending the Civil Rights Act to protect against discrimination for organizing presents an easily understandable idea that is much less susceptible to distortion by opponents. The simple message: people should not be fired for trying to organize a union and join the middle class.

Because the legislation would not address the various issues of elections and arbitration and the inner workings of the NLRB, the bill would avoid questions about secret ballot elections and union behavior, instead isolating the straight-forward issue of employer behavior. And by focusing on the ability of *individuals* to protect themselves from wrongful termination, the legislation underlines the David and Goliath nature of the conflict between large employers and individual employees. The contest between a few individuals and the firm may paint a more sympathetic picture for some than the battle between an employer and a union. And the legislation would remind people that it is individual workers choosing to exercise their right to organize in pursuit of better conditions who pay the price when employers unfairly use their economic power to stop unions.

Likewise, emphasizing the simple issue of employer discrimination is likely to be appealing to many Americans, whether or not they like labor unions. Americans believe quite strongly that employment discrimination is wrong, even when they are not particularly sympathetic to the group of individuals who are the victims of discrimination. For example, in 2000, only 28.8 percent of Americans approved of sexual relations between adults of the same sex, yet in the same year, 75.3 percent supported laws protecting gays and lesbians from employment discrimination.[14] So iconic is the idea of nondiscrimination that when Kentucky U.S. Senate candidate Rand Paul raised questions about the Civil Rights Act from a libertarian perspective in the 2010 election, suggesting the law interfered too heavily with private enterprise, he was forced to hastily recant.[15]

Of course, the downside of the simple approach to labor law reform is that the legislation covers fewer employer abuses. Amending the civil rights law will not completely level the playing field between labor and management, because it fails to address a number of employer practices that hurt unions. It will not provide enhanced penalties for threatening to close down a unionized plant, address delays in elections, the practice of permanently replacing striking workers, the ban on secondary boycotts, or failure of employers to negotiate once a union is certified.[16]

These are all important issues that should be addressed. But the civil rights approach would take a very substantial first step by removing what evidence suggests is the most powerful weapon an employer has to end a union drive: firing a few employees who support the union and terrorizing the rest into submission.[17] As Geoghegan notes, "the main reason" employers can stop union drives, even when a majority of employees want to join a union, is that "employers can pick out and fire all the hard-core pro-union workers." He continues, "Union busting now is almost a science. And the science is a pretty simple one: You go out and fire people. And keep firing until the organizing stops. Because at some point it always will. It is like sending people straight into a machine gun, and when the bodies pile up high enough, the drive is over and the employer has won."[18] Rational employees who have responsibilities to feed their families eventually get the message and stop agitating. Taking away this powerful employer weapon is absolutely critical, and because the issue presented is a simple one, the legislation has a far better chance of passing quickly than more comprehensive reform.

Emphasizing Values over Interests

Connecting labor organizing to the civil rights movement could also broaden appeal, particularly among progressives and young people, who are yearning to be part of something bigger than just themselves. As long as conservatives try to paint unions as greedy self-interested institutions— "special interests" just after their slice of the pie—labor law reform is unlikely to spark a romantic association for progressives.

Framing labor as part of the larger civil rights struggle underlines the reality that labor helps lead America's broad movement for social change, aiding union members and nonmembers alike. While labor is appropriately committed to higher wages and better working conditions for its members, it is also part of a bigger social justice movement that fights for equality across the board, championing stronger health care, education, and minimum wage policies that help all Americans.

In the past, the fact that labor was part of the heroic fight for economic justice was self-evident, as the names John L. Lewis and Norma Rae had broad resonance with the American public.[19] But few Americans are today deeply familiar with the history of the labor movement.[20] And as organized labor shrinks as a proportion of the workforce, fewer and fewer young people have fathers, mothers, aunts, uncles, or neighbors who can educate them about the labor movement's considerable accomplishments in the fight for a fairer society.

By contrast, Americans know well the glorious history and accomplishments of the black freedom and civil rights movement. A 2004 CNN/AARP poll found that 81 percent of Americans rate the civil rights movement as "extremely important" or "very important."[21] For many progressives, the civil rights era is part of the "golden age" of liberal activism in which individuals came together to fight to rectify long-standing injustices. Not surprisingly, the civil rights movement is routinely invoked when leaders are trying to motivate audiences to act for a particular cause. Presidents George W. Bush and Barack Obama both, for example, have called education reform the "civil rights issue of our time."[22] Writing labor organizing into the Civil Rights Act would help underline the deep historical ties between the civil rights and labor movements as what King called "the two most dynamic and cohesive liberal forces in the country."[23]

The Broad Appeal of Individual Rights

In addition, conceiving of labor organizing as a civil right conforms better to America's Emersonian belief in individualism than does labor's traditional appeal to solidarity. While there is a great deal to be said for labor's strong support for collective action, it has always stood in tension with America's deeply held belief in individual rights.[24] The civil rights approach to protecting labor turns this political liability on its head by tapping into the strong American belief in the rights of individuals.

Public opinion polling has long found that Americans are more ardent believers in individual rights than are citizens of other nations. For example, Americans are far more supportive of individual rights of freedom of expression, including offensive speech, than are those in other countries. According to 2009 poll of citizens in twenty nations, on average, 57 percent agreed that "people should be allowed to publicly criticize a religion because people should have freedom of speech" while 34 percent instead said that governments "should have the right to fine or imprison people who publicly criticize a religion because such criticism could defame the religion." The 23-point margin in support of free speech in the twenty countries compared with a towering 80-point margin in the United States, where 89 percent supported the right to criticize religion compared to 9 percent who supported government restrictions. The U.S. support for free speech rights was the highest of all twenty countries, outstripping even European democracies such as the United Kingdom (81 percent support), Germany (76 percent), and France (66 percent).[25]

Indeed, asked to define "the most important role for government," a 2010 Rasmussen poll of likely voters found that when given three choices, 59 percent of Americans responded "to protect individual rights and freedom," compared with 24 percent who suggested government's primary role is "to ensure fairness and social justice" and 10 percent who said it is "to manage the economy."[26] A government law to protect a lone individual trying to stand up for her right to join a union against the power of an employer fits nicely into this paradigm.

Conservative opponents of labor have long understood the rhetorical power of rights, employing "right to work" as the slogan for state laws that forbid workers from having to pay for benefits associated with collective bargaining agreements. These laws in fact have nothing to do with a right to work; they are really a right to free ride off the efforts of others. Indeed, because these laws in practice make it harder for unions to survive and weaken their presence, labor supporters say they provide the "right to work for less."[27] Organized labor would be wise to take back the rhetoric of rights from those who in reality are opposed to expanding rights for working people.

Combining the Popularity of Rights with the Popularity of Populism

A policy proposal for stronger unions connected to civil rights may find a particularly receptive audience, as Americans show growing dissatisfaction with rising economic inequality, wage stagnation, and a shrinking of the American middle class. Polls find Americans are increasingly supportive of government action that will reduce economic inequality. A 2011 NBC/*Wall Street Journal* poll, for example, found that, by 76 percent to 12 percent, Americans agreed, "The current economic structure of the country is out of balance and favors a very small proportion of the rich over the rest of the country. America needs to reduce the power of major banks and corporations and demand greater accountability and transparency. The government should not provide financial aid to corporations and should not provide tax breaks to the rich."[28] A 2011 *New York Times*/CBS poll, likewise, found that 66 percent of Americans say that the nation's wealth should be more evenly distributed.[29]

Of the various options for reducing inequality, increasing government welfare programs is unpopular on three fronts: it does not reward hard work, it increases the budget deficit, and it is run by "government," which remains suspect in the eyes of many. According to a December 2011 Gallup poll, for example, 64 percent said "big government" is the "biggest threat to the country," compared to 26 percent who identified "big business" and just 8 percent who identified "big labor."[30]

Legislation to reduce inequality by strengthening private sector unions, by contrast, uses a nongovernmental entity to produce more widely shared gains, rewards only those who are working, and does not cost the public treasury. As Geoghegan notes, "The whole thing is free. It's entirely off budget. It doesn't add a single penny to the deficit."[31] When unions win concessions from private sector corporations to share in productivity gains, Geoghegan notes, "taxpayers are off the hook because the employer provides the safety net."[32]

Polls also suggest Americans are looking for institutions to serve as a check on corporate power and wealth in the political sphere. As we noted in chapter 2, a 2011 *New York Times*/CBS News poll found that not only do 69 percent think the Republicans favor the rich, but a plurality think the Democratic administration of Barack Obama favors the rich as well.[33] Unions are well positioned to play this counterbalancing role, which helps explain general public support for organized labor. A 2005 CNN/Gallup/*USA Today* survey, for example, found that Americans generally side with unions over employers in labor disputes. When asked "In the labor disputes of the last two or three years, have your sympathies in general been on the side of unions or on the side of the companies?" 52 percent said the unions, while only 34 percent said the companies.[34] Meanwhile, as noted in chapter 3, in 2005 Americans were 43 percentage points more likely to approve than disapprove of unions.[35]

Combining the invocation of "rights" with the country's populist mood may help explain the lopsided poll results when the question of "collective bargaining rights" for public employees is posed. Following efforts by Republicans in Wisconsin to curtail collective bargaining rights for teachers and other public employees, a 2011 NBC/*Wall Street Journal* poll found that, by 62 percent to 33 percent, voters opposed eliminating public employees' "collective-bargaining rights." The same poll found that 77 percent believed public employees should "have the same collective-bargaining rights" as unionized private sector workers.[36] In the November 2011 Ohio election, voters supported, by 61 percent 39 percent, a repeal of Republican governor John Kasich's effort to reduce collective bargaining rights for public employees. The support for collective bargaining rights was overwhelming, even though the Ohio electorate was hardly left-wing, simultaneously supporting a symbolic measure to disapprove of national legislation requiring individuals to purchase health insurance by a very wide margin.[37]

All in all, there are reasons to think that, with a smart strategy—one that isolates the issue of abusive employer behavior, emphasizes that important values are at stake, and is tied to deeply held American beliefs about individual rights—improvements to union organizing rights could be legislated in the United States. Business will fight reform every step of the way, but a fresh civil rights approach, coupled with deep public concerns about inequality and the shrinking middle class, could provide a winning strategy the next time Democrats take political control in Washington.

Conclusion

For the past half century, labor law reform has failed time and time again. As a result, unions have shrunk and inequality has soared to record heights, squeezing the American middle class and fundamentally altering the balance in our democracy. The evidence from other wealthy nations that have healthy labor movements suggests that the deunionization of the American workforce is not inevitable but rather in large measure is the result of weak laws.

Just as civil rights groups historically drew upon the tactics and methods of labor, so too, today, the trade union movement should draw inspiration from the remarkable gains of black Americans following passage of the Civil Rights Act. The language of the NLRA and the UN Declaration of Human Rights with respect to organizing is largely meaningless so long as employers can stymie union drives by firing key employees and intimidating the rest.

In a time of growing inequality and tight budgets, when Americans are looking for ways to rebuild our middle-class democracy, we need to think fresh about how to give average Americans a genuine right to band together and pursue their interests and values in the workplace and in the halls of Congress. This country made enormous advances when Americans decided as a society to make race and sex discrimination illegal. If we want the labor movement to rejoin civil rights groups in what Martin Luther King Jr. called a powerful coalition to be "architects of democracy," we need to be sure that labor, too, is protected from discrimination through our civil rights laws.

Notes

Chapter One

1. Digital Library of Georgia, "Memphis Sanitation Workers Strike," The Civil Rights Digital Library, http://crdl.usg.edu/events/memphis_sanitation_strike/?Welcome.

2. Martin Luther King, Jr., *All Labor Has Dignity,* ed. Michael K. Honey (Boston: Beacon Press, 2011), 167–68; *I Am a Man,* documentary film (Memphis, Tenn.: Memphis Tourism Foundation, 2009).

3. *All Labor Has Dignity,* xvii, xxxv, and 172–74.

4. *All Labor Has Dignity,* 38.

5. Kim Bobo, "King's More Perfect Unions," Religion Dispatches, January 14, 2011, http://www.religiondispatches.org/books/politics/4051/king%E2%80%99s_more_perfect_unions/ .

6. Stephen B. Oates, *Let the Trumpet Sound: The Life of Martin Luther King , Jr.* (New York: New American Library, 1982), 434–45.

7. King, address to AFSME, March 18, 1968, in *All Labor Has Dignity,* 174–75.

8. The proportion of lawyers and doctors who are African American has increased significantly during the civil rights era. For increases since 1983, see U.S. Bureau of Labor Statistics, Household Data Annual Averages, "11. Employed Persons by Detailed Occupation, Sex, Race, and Hispanic or Latino Ethnicity," 1983, 1996, ftp://ftp.bls.gov/pub/special.requests/lf/AA96/aat11.txt, and 2010, http://www.bls.gov/cps/cpsaat11.pdf. Likewise, the black/white gap in high school attainment among adults age twenty-five and over shrunk from 21.3 percentage points in 1970 to just 7.5 points in 2010. See U.S. Department of Education, Digest of Education Statistics: 2010, "Table 8. Percentage of Persons Age 25 and Over and 25 to 29, by Race/Ethnicity, Years of School Completed, and Sex: Selected Years, 1910 through 2010," http://nces.ed.gov/programs/digest/d10/tables/dt10_008.asp.

9. Randall Kennedy, *The Persistence of the Color Line: Racial Politics and the Obama Presidency* (New York: Pantheon Books, 2011), 233.

10. For a fascinating account of how the American civil rights movement affected the Indian struggle against imperialism and caste distinctions, see Nico Slate, *Colored Cosmopolitanism* (Cambridge: Harvard University Press, 2012).

11. Bureau of Labor Statistics, "Union Members—2010," January 21, 2011, http://www.bls.gov/news.release/union2.nr0.htm; *All Labor Has Dignity*, xxii.

12. Arthur B. Kennickell, "Ponds and Streams: Wealth and Income in the U.S., 1989 to 2007," Finance and Economics Discussion Series, Divisions of Research & Statistics and Monetary Affairs, Federal Reserve Board, Washington, D.C., January 9, 2009, 35, Table 4 (on wealth) http://www.federalreserve.gov/pubs/feds/2009/200913/200913pap.pdf]; Ian Dew-Becker and Robert J. Gordon, "Where Did the Productivity Growth Go? Inflation Dynamics and the Distribution of Income," Brookings Panel on Economic Activity, 2005, 2 (on income from 1966 to 2001).

13. See chapter 2.

14. See David Segal, "Lawyers Stake a Claim on Bias Lawsuits," *Washington Post,* January 27, 1997, A1.

15. Thomas Geoghegan, *Which Side Are You On? Trying to Be for Labor When It's Flat on Its Back* (New York: Farrar, Straus and Giroux, 1991), 255.

16. Steven Greenhouse, "Labor Campaign Highlights Workers' Right to Unionize," *New York Times,* June 25, 1998, A12.

17. Taylor E. Dark III, "Prospects for Labor Law Reform," *Perspectives on Work* (Summer 2008/Winter 2009): 24, http://www.lera.uiuc.edu/pubs/perspectives/Comp Articles/TDexcerpt.pdf.

18. Quoted in David Byrd, "A Slave to Stalemate," *National Journal,* September 4, 1999, p. 2487.

19. See, e.g., Mark Murray, "NBC/WSJ poll: 62% against Stripping Public Employees' Bargaining Rights," (by 62-33%, Americans oppose eliminating public employees' collective-bargaining rights; and 77 percent say that public employees should have the same collective-bargaining rights as employees in the private sector), http://first read.msnbc.msn.com/_news/2011/03/02/6171265-nbcwsj-poll-62-against-stripping-public-employees-bargaining-rights.

20. See chapter 2.

21. George Packer, "The Broken Contract: Inequality and American Decline," *Foreign Affairs,* November/December 2011.

22. Robert Reich, "The Truth About the American Economy," May 30, 2011, http://robertreich.org/post/5993482080.

23. See, e.g., Eric Foner, in Steven Greenhouse, "Liberal Academics and Labor's New Leaders Pulling in Tandem Once More," *New York Times,* September 22, 1996, 36.

24. Geoghegan, *Which Side Are You On?* 50–51.

25. John B. Judis, "Collective Bargain: As Wisconsin Goes, So Goes the Nation," *The New Republic,* March 3, 2011, http://www.tnr.com/article/politics/magazine/84501/wisconsin-unions-collective-bargaining.

26. Reich, "The Truth About the American Economy."

27. For evidence regarding these three propositions, see chapter 2.

28. Richard B. Freeman, "Do Workers Still Want Unions? More Than Ever," EPI Briefing Paper 182, Economic Policy Institute, 2007, http://www.sharedprosperity.org/bp182/bp182.pdf.

29. Edward Epstein, "House Passes Pro-Labor Bill to Help Workers Form Unions," *San Francisco Chronicle,* March 2, 2007 (re 2005 figure).; Gerald Mayer, "Union Membership Trends in the United States," Congressional Research Service, 2004, 22–23, http://digitalcommons.ilr.cornell.edu/cgi/viewcontent.cgi?article=1176&context=key_workplace (re 1950s).

30. Kate Bronfenbrenner, "No Holds Barred—The Intensification of Employer Opposition to Organizing," Economic Policy Institute, May 20, 2009, 23, http://www.epi.org/publications/entry/bp235.

31. John Schmitt and Ben Zipperer, "Dropping the Ax: Illegal Firings during Union Election Campaigns," Center for Economic and Policy Research, January 2007, 1.

32. *Seventy-Fourth Annual Report of the National Labor Relations Board for the Fiscal Year Ended September 30, 2009* (Washington, D.C.: National Labor Relations Board, February 23, 2010), Table 23.

33. Ibid., Table 4.

34. Hendrik Hertzberg, "Labor's China Syndrome," *The New Yorker*, June 5, 2000, 31.

35. Charles J. Morris, "A Tale of Two Statutes: Discrimination for Union Activity Under the NLRA and RLA," *Employee Rights and Employment Policy Journal* 2 (1998): 319.

36. Jeffrey M. Hirsch and Barry T. Hirsch, "The Rise and Fall of Private Sector Unionism: What Next for the NLRA? *Florida State University Law Review* 34 (2007): 1180; see also Union Membership and Coverage Database, Union Membership, Coverage, Density and Employment by Industry (2006), www.unionstats.com.

37. Quoted in Lisa Belkin, "The Union Kids," *New York Times Magazine*, January 21, 1996, 38.

38. The Universal Declaration of Human Rights, Article 23, www.un.org/en/documents/udhr. See also chapter 4.

39. See, e.g., Theodore J. St. Antoine, "Federal Regulation of the Workplace in the Next Half Century." *Chicago-Kent Law Review* 61 (1985): 639, http://heinonline.org/HOL/Page?collection=journals&handle=hein.journals/chknt61&id=643; John Logan, "Union Recognition and Collective Bargaining: How Does the United States Compare with Other Democracies?" *Academics on Employee Free Choice* (Berkeley: University of California–Berkeley Center for Labor Research and Education, 2009), 48.

40. *The Global State of Workers' Rights: Free Labor in a Hostile World* (New York: Freedom House, August 2010), 10.

41. Halley Potter, conversation with Marick F. Masters, Wayne State University, January 6, 2012. See also Mavick F. Masters and Robert S. Atkin, "The Finances of Major Unions," *Industrial Relations* 36, no. 4 (October 1997): 494, table 1 (estimating real revenue of all U.S. unions to be $8.4 billion in 1995).

42. See, e.g., W. Mark Crain and Joseph M. Johnson, "Compliance Costs of Federal Workplace Regulations: Survey Results for U.S. Manufacturers," December 2001, http://mercatus.org/uploadedFiles/Mercatus/Publications/MC_RSP_RA-Workplace Survey_001201.pdf; Karen O'Leonard and Stacey Harris, *The HR Factbook 2011* (Oakland, Calif.: Bersin & Associates, June 2011), http://marketing.bersin.com/rs/bersin/images/060111_ES_HRFactbook_KOL_Final.pdf; and Sara E. Savage, "HR Spending on the Increase," Human Resource Executive Online, June 21, 2006, http://www.hreonline.com/HRE/story.jsp?storyId=5690104.

43. Cited in Thomas Frank, "It's Time to Give Voters the Liberalism They Want," *Wall Street Journal*, November 19, 2008.

44. See *NAACP v. Alabama*, 357 U.S. 449 (1958).

45. See chapter 5.

46. Julian Bond, "Labor Rights Are Civil Rights," excerpts from address to the AFL-CIO, July 2005. See also Richard B. Freeman and Joel Rogers, *What Workers*

Want (Ithaca, N.Y.: ILR Press, 1999), 71 (59 percent of blacks, compared with 28 percent of nonblacks, would vote for a union if given a chance).

47. "Table 5. Union Affiliation of Employed Wage and Salary Workers by State," U.S. Bureau of Labor Statistics, http://www.bls.gov/news.release/union2.t05.htm.

48. Michael Honey, "Operation Dixie: Labor and Civil Rights in the Postwar South," *The Mississippi Quarterly* (1992), http://www.thefreelibrary.com/Operation +Dixie%3A+labor+and+civil+rights+in+the+Postwar+South.-a013784480.

49. Richard L. Berke, "Chasing the Polls on Gay Rights," *New York Times,* August 2, 1998, sec. 4, 3.

50. "Majority of Voters Say Protecting Individual Rights Is Government's Chief Role," Rasmussen Reports, http://www.rasmussenreports.com/public_content/politics/ general_politics/december_2010/majority_of_voters_say_protecting_individual_ rights_is_government_s_chief_role. By contrast, 24 percent believe a government's primary purpose is to ensure fairness and social justice, while 10 percent say it is to manage the economy.

51. Greenhouse, "Labor Campaign Highlights Workers' Right to Unionize," A12.

52. Geoghegan, *Which Side Are You On?* 269.

Chapter Two

1. See, e.g., Gerald Friedman, "Labor Unions in the United States," Economic History Association, http://eh.net/encyclopedia/article/friedman.unions.us; and Thomas Geoghegan, *Which Side Are You On? Trying to Be for Labor When It's Flat on Its Back* (New York: Farrar, Straus and Giroux, 1991), 23, 42.

2. Gerald Mayer, "Union Membership Trends in the United States," Congressional Research Service, 2004, 22–23, http://digitalcommons.ilr.cornell.edu/cgi/view content.cgi?article=1176&context=key_workplace; and Martin Luther King, Jr., *All Labor Has Dignity,* ed. Michael K. Honey (Boston: Beacon Press, 2011), xxii.

3. "Union Members—2010," Bureau of Labor Statistics, table 2, January 21, 2011, available at http://www.bls.gov/news.release/union2.nr0.htm. The wage premium in earlier times of higher union density was estimated to be one-third. See *What's Next for Organized Labor? Report of The Century Foundation Task Force on the Future of Unions* (New York: The Century Foundation Press, 1999), 7–8.

4. John Schmitt, *The Union of the States* (Washington: Center for Economic and Policy Research, February 2010),15, 18.

5. Colvin, Alexander, Rosemary Batt, and Harry Katz, "How High Performance Human Resource Practices and Workforce Unionization Affect Managerial Pay," Articles and Chapters, Paper 274, 2001, 24 http://digitalcommons.ilr.cornell.edu/cgi/ viewcontent.cgi?article=1276&context=articles&sei-redir=1.

6. "Employee Benefits in the United States," Bureau of Labor Statistics, tables 2, 5, and 6. www.bls.gov/ncs/ebs/sp/ebnr0016.pdf.

7. Ibid., tables 3 and 4.

8. Lawrence Mishel and Matthew Walter, "How Unions Help All Workers," Economic Policy Institute, 2003, table 4, http://www.epi.org/page/-/old/briefing papers/143/bp143.pdf.

9. Yu Hsing, "A Macroeconomic Analysis of the Impact of Union Wage Increases on Nonunion Wages," *Applied Economics Letters* 8, no. 12 (2010): 806.

10. *What's Next for Organized Labor?* 12.

11. Henry S. Farber, "Nonunion Wage Rates and the Threat of Unionization," *Industrial and Labor Relations Review* 58, no. 3 (April 2005), cited in David Madland, Karla Walter, and Nick Bunker, "Unions Make the Middle Class: Without Unions, the Middle Class Withers," Center for American Progress, April 2011, 6.

12. Chang Hwan Kim and Arthur Sakamoto, "The Rise of Intra-Occupational Wage Inequality in the United States," *American Sociological Review* 73, no. 1 (2008): 150; see also Lawrence Mishel, and Ross Eisenbrey, "Union Declines Hurt All Workers," *Salt Lake Tribune* (Salt Lake City), December 12, 2005, http://www.epi.org/publications/entry/webfeatures_viewpoints_union_decline/ .

13. Robert Reich, "The Truth About the American Economy," May 30, 2011, available at http://robertreich.org/post/5993482080; Madland et al., "Unions Make the Middle Class," 6.

14. Randall Garton, "Collective Bargaining Teaches Democratic Values, Activism," Shanker Blog, September 16, 2011, http://shankerblog.org/?p=3716. Likewise, for the role of unions in promoting civic participating, see Robert Putnam, "Bowling Alone: America's Declining Social Capital," interview, http://xroads.virginia.edu/~HYPER/DETOC/assoc/bowling.html.

15. Emily Sherman, "AFL-CIO Kicks Off Largest Get Out the Vote Effort Ever," CNN, http://politicalticker.blogs.cnn.com/2008/10/21/afl-cio-kicks-off-largest-get-out-the-vote-effort-ever/.

16. James Parks, "Trumka: Be Proud of Union GOTV Effort," AFL-CIO NOW Blog, http://blog.aflcio.org/2010/11/03/trumka-be-proud-of-union-gotv-effort-get-ready-again-to-fight-for-jobs/.

17. Madland et al., "Unions Make the Middle Class," 15, citing Benjamin Radcliffe and Patricia Davis, "Labor Organization and Electoral Participation in Industrial Democracies," *American Journal of Political Science* 44, no. 1 (2000): 132–41.

18. Roland Zullo, "Union Cities and Voter Turnout," Labor and Employment Relations Association Series, Proceedings of 58th Annual Meeting, Champaign, Ill., 2006, cited in Madland et al., "Unions Make the Middle Class," 15.

19. The Center for Responsive Politics, "Top All-Time Donors," Open Secrets, http://www.opensecrets.org/orgs/ list.php.

20. Spencer MacColl, "Citizens United Decision Profoundly Affects Political Landscape," The Center for Responsive Politics, Slide 7, http://www.opensecrets.org/news/2011/05/citizens-united-decision-profoundly-affects-political-landscape.html.

21. Associated Press, "Unions Defend Costly Attempt to Oust Lincoln," MSNBC, June 9, 2010, http://www.msnbc.msn.com/id/ 37577406/ns/politics-decision_2010/t/unions-defend-costly-attempt-oust-lincoln/.

22. Spencer MacColl, Slide 7.

23. Roland Zullo, "Union Membership and Political Inclusion," *Industrial and Labor Relations Review* 62, no. 1 (2008): 33.

24. Harold Meyerson, "A Post Election Numbers Game," *Washington Post,* November 5, 2010.

25. Julius G. Getman, *Restoring the Power of Unions: It Takes a Movement,* (New Haven, CT: Yale University Press, 2010), 16.

26. Reich, "The Truth About the American Economy."

27. Jacob S. Hacker and Paul Pierson, *Winner-Take-All Politics: How Washington Made the Rich Richer—and Turned Its Back on the Middle Class* (New York: Simon & Schuster, 2010), 139. See also Michael Lind, "Liberalism and the Post-union Future,"

Salon, February 22, 2011, http://www.salon.com/news/politics/war_room/2011/02/22/lind_unions_wisconsin; and Kenneth A. Germanson, "Labor History Primer," Wisconsin Labor History Society, http://www.wisconsinlaborhistory.org/?page_id=34.

28. Jacob S. Hacker and Paul Pierson, "The Wisconsin Union Fight Isn't About Benefits, It's About Labor's Influence," *Washington Post,* March 6, 2011, http://www.washingtonpost.com/wp-dyn/content/article/2011/03/04/AR20110 30406264.html.

29. Jill S. Quadagno, "Organized Labor's Health Benefits," in *One Nation, Uninsured: Why the U.S. Has No National Health Insurance* (New York: Oxford University Press, 2005), 76.

30. Steven Greenhouse, "Labor Leaders and Intellectuals Are Forging New Alliance," *New York Times,* September 22, 1996, http://www.writing.upenn.edu/~afilreis/50s/labor-intellectuals.html.

31. Thomas Geoghegan, *Which Side Are You On?* 50–51.

32. Shanker, quoted in Richard D. Kahlenberg, *Tough Liberal: Albert Shanker and the Battles Over Schools, Unions, Race, and Democracy* (New York: Columbia University Press, 2007), 207.

33. Agence France-Presse, "Republicans Attack Unions to Hurt Democrats: Analysts," The Raw Story, http://www.rawstory.com/rs/2011/02/19/republicans-attack-unions-to-hurt-democrats-analysts/.

34. John B. Judis, "Collective Bargain: As Wisconsin Goes, So Goes the Nation," *The New Republic,* March 3, 2011, http://www.tnr.com/article/politics/magazine/84501/wisconsin-unions-collective-bargaining.

35. Bureau of Labor Statistics, "Union Members—2010." For a discussion on the symbolic effect of President Reagan's firing the air traffic controllers, see Damon A. Silvers, "How a Low Wage Economy with Weak Labor Laws Brought Us the Mortgage Credit Crisis," *Berkeley Journal Employment and Labor Law* 29 (2008): 455–72.

36. Barry Hirsch and David Macpherson, "IV. Industry: Union Membership, Coverage, Density, and Employment by Industry, 1983-2010," Union Membership and Coverage Database, http://unionstats.gsu.edu/.

37. Bureau of Labor Statistics, "Union Members—2010."

38. See "Trends in the Distribution of Household Income Between 1979 and 2007," Congressional Budget Office, October 2011; and Robert Pear, "Top Earners Doubled Share of Nation's Income, Study Finds," *New York Times,* October 25, 2011. See also Aviva Aron-Dine and Arloc Sherman, "New CBO Data Show Income Inequality Continues to Widen," Center on Budget and Policy Priorities, January 23, 2007, http://www.cbpp.org/cms/?fa=view&id=957.

39. Jia Lynn Yang and Erica W. Morrison, "Americans Dip into Savings as Their Incomes Decline," *Washington Post,* October 1, 2011, A11.

40. See Josh Bivins, "CEOs Distance Themselves from the Average Worker," Economic Snapshot, Economic Policy Institute, November 9, 2011.

41. See "Trends in the Distribution of Household Income Between 1979 and 2007," Congressional Budget Office, October 2011; and Robert Pear, "Top Earners Doubled Share of Nation's Income, Study Finds," *New York Times,* October 25, 2011. See also Emmanuel Saez and Thomas Piketty, "Income Inequality in the United States, 1913–1998 (Updated 2008)," *Quarterly Journal of Economics* 118, no. 1 (2003): 1–39, Table B-2, http://emlab.berkeley.edu/users/saez/pikettyqje.pdf.

42. Sylvia A. Allegretto, "The State of Working America's Wealth, 2011," The Economic Policy Institute, 6, table 3, and 7, figure C, www.epi.org/page/-/Briefing Paper292.pdf.

43. Robert Frank, "Billionaires Own as Much as the Bottom Half of Americans?" *Wall Street Journal,* March 7, 2011.

44. "No Matter How You Slice It, Compensation Is Not Keeping Up with Productivity, Economic Policy Institute," cited in Madland et al., "Unions Make the Middle Class," 7. See also Lawrence Mishel and Heidi Shierholz, "The Sad but True Story of Wages in America," Economic Policy Institute, 2011, 1, http://www.epi.org/page/-/old/Issuebriefs/IssueBrief297.pdf?nocdn=1.

45. Ian Dew-Becker and Robert J. Gordon, "Where Did the Productivity Growth Go? Inflation Dynamics and the Distribution of Income," Brookings Panel on Economic Activity, 2005, 2.

46. Madland et al., "Unions Make the Middle Class," 3, 23.

47. Martin A. Asher and Robert H. DeFina, "The Impact of Changing Union Density on Earnings Inequality: Evidence from the Private and Public Sectors," *Journal of Labor Research* 18, no. 3 (1997): 425, http://www.springerlink.com/content/br5hj20465165270/fulltext.pdf.

48. Cited in Benjamin Landy, Graph of the Day, The Century Foundation, November 2, 2011, http://botc.tcf.org/2011/11/graph-of-the-day-has-the-decline-of-unions-made-america-less-equal-.html. See also Madland et al., "Unions Make the Middle Class," 25. Even Ben Bernanke suggests that declining union membership "can explain between 10 and 20 percent of the rise in wage inequality among men during the 1970s and 1980s," quoted in Madland et al., "Unions Make the Middle Class," 23.

49. Sheldon, Danziger, Peter Gottschalk, and Richard B Freeman, "How Much Has De-Unionization Contributed to the Rise in Male Earnings Inequality?" in *Uneven Tides: Rising Inequality in America* (New York: Russell Sage Foundation, 1993), 134.

50. Hacker and Pierson, *Winner-Take-All Politics,* 142, citing Richard B. Freeman, "What Do Unions Do to Voting?" NBER Working Paper no. 9992 (September 2003).

51. Hacker and Pierson, *Winner-Take-All Politics,* 99–100.

52. David Broder, "The Price of Labor's Decline," *Washington Post,* September 9, 2004, A27.

53. New York Times/CBS News Poll, October 19–24, 2011, http://s3.documentcloud.org/documents/259646/the-new-york-times-cbs-news-poll-oct-2011.pdf (finding that 28 percent say the policies of the Obama administration "favor the rich" compared with 23 percent saying they "favor the middle class," 17 percent "favor the poor," and 21 percent "treat all groups equally") See also Michael Tomasky, "Rich Man Rules," *The Daily Beast,* October 26, 2011.

54. Hacker and Pierson, *Winner-Take-All Politics,* 52, citing Thomas L. Hungerford, "Income Inequality, Income Mobility and Economic Policy," CRS Report for Congress, April 4, 2008.

55. Madland et al., "Unions Make the Middle Class," 3. See also ibid, 25.

56. See, e.g., Arthur S. Alderson and Francois Nielsen, "Globalization and the Great U-Turn: Income Inequality Trends in 16 OECD Countries," *American Journal of Sociology* 107, no. 5 (2002): 1244–99 (noting Freeman's research finding that in examining workers in sixteen OECD countries across the 1980s, "the upswing in earnings inequality at the industry level was least pronounced in highly unionized countries").

57. Jelle Visser, "Union Membership Statistics in 24 Countries," *Monthly Labor Review* 129, no. 1 (January 2006): 42, http://www.bls.gov/opub/mlr/2006/01/art3full.pdf.

58. John Schmitt and Alexandra Mitukiewicz, "Politics Matters: Changes in Unionization Rates in Rich Countries, 1960–2010," Center for Economic and Policy Research, November 2011, Figure 2, 5.

59. James B. Davies, Susanna Sandstrom, Anthony Shorrocks, and Edward N. Wolff, "The World Distribution of Household Wealth," Personal Assets from a Global Perspective (Conference), 2007, Table 3, http://escholarship.org/uc/item/3jv048hx#page-11.

60. "Distribution of Family Income: Gini Index," CIA World Factbook, https://www.cia.gov/library/publications/the-world-factbook/fields/2172.html.

61. See, e.g., Michael Gerson, "Moving on Up: It's Social Mobility, Not Income Inequality, That Matters Most," *Washington Post,* November 4, 2011.

62. See Paul Krugman, "The Great Gatsby Curve," *New York Times,* January 15, 2012, http://krugman.blogs.nytimes.com/2012/01/15/the-great-gatsby-curve/ (referencing Alan Kreuger's data).

63. Hacker and Pierson, *Winner-Take-All Politics,* 28–29.

64. Julia Isaacs, The Brookings Institution, cited in Harold Meyerson, "No Longer a Land of Opportunity," *Washington Post,* January 4, 2012. See also Jason DeParle, "Harder for Americans to Rise from Lower Rungs," *New York Times,* January 5, 2012.

65. Ibid., 79–80.

66. Spence, quoted in Nicholas D. Kristof, "Occupy the Agenda," *New York Times,* November 20, 2011.

67. See, e.g., Reich, "The Truth About the American Economy." See also David Madland, "Growth and the Middle Class," *Democracy Journal,* Spring 2011, 16–22 (explaining the several ways in which a strong middle class promotes economic growth).

68. See, e.g., Thomas Geoghegan, *Were You Born on the Wrong Continent? How the European Model Can Help You Get a Life* (New York: New Press, 2010), 156; and Meyerson, "No Longer the Land of Opportunity" (suggesting Germany has "the most successful economy in the advanced industrial world").

69. Hacker and Pierson, *Winner-Take-All Politics,* 15–16.

Chapter Three

1. Matthew J. Slaughter, "Globalization and Declining Unionization in the United States," *Industrial Relations: A Journal of Economy and Society* 46, no. 2 (April, 2007): 329–46. Kate Bronfenbrenner, *Uneasy Terrain: The Impact of Capital Mobility on Workers, Wages, and Union Organizing* [Electronic version] (Ithaca, N.Y.: Author, 2000), http://digitalcommons.ilr.cornell.edu/reports/3/. John Schmitt and Alexandra Mitukiewicz, "Politics Matter: Changes in Unionization Rates in Rich Countries, 1960–2010," Center for Economic and Policy Research, November 2011, 2–3, http://www.cepr.net/index.php/publications/reports/changes-in-unionization-rates-in-rich-countries-1960-2010.

2. Schmitt and Mitukiewicz, "Politics Matter," 2 (describing the view but not subscribing to it.)

3. Ibid.

4. Ibid., 3.

5. Ibid., 3.

6. John Logan, "Union Recognition and Collective Bargaining: How Does the United States Compare with Other Democracies?" in *Academics on Employee Free Choice* (Berkeley, Calif.: University of California–Berkeley Center for Labor Research and Education, 2009), 47.

7. W. Craig Riddell, "Unionization in Canada and the United States: A Tale of Two Countries," in *Small Differences That Matter: Labor Markets and Income Maintenance in Canada and the United States,* ed. David Card and Richard Freeman

(Chicago: Chicago University Press and National Bureau of Economic Research, 1993): 109–48, cited in Jacob S. Hacker and Paul Pierson, *Winner-Take-All Politics: How Washington Made the Rich Richer—and Turned Its Back on the Middle Class* (New York: Simon & Schuster, 2010), 60–61.

8. Richard B. Freeman, "Do Workers Still Want Unions? More Than Ever," EPI Briefing Paper 182, 2007, 6–7, http://www.sharedprosperity.org/bp182/bp182.pdf.

9. See David Madland and Karla Walter, "Why Is the Public Suddenly Down on Unions? The Bad Economy's to Blame—Support Should Recover When the Economy Does," Center for American Progress, July 2010.

10. Ibid., 7 (in the poll, 30 percent wanted less influence for unions).

11. Gallup Poll, cited in Ed Rogers, "Obama's Misstep on Class Warfare," *Washington Post,* December 15, 2011 (64 percent said "big government" is the "biggest threat to the country," compared to 26 percent who identified "big business" and just 8 percent who identified "big labor").

12. Freeman, "Do Workers Still Want Unions?" 2.

13. Ibid., 3.

14. Paul Weiler, "Promises to Keep: Securing Workers' Rights to Self-Organization under the NLRA," *Harvard Law Review* 96, no. 8 (1983): 1769–80. See also Hacker and Pierson, *Winner-Take-All Politics,* 128; and Thomas Geoghegan, *Which Side Are You On? Trying to Be for Labor When It's Flat on Its Back* (New York: Farrar, Straus and Giroux, 1991), 254.

15. Paul Weiler, cited in *What's Next for Organized Labor? Report of The Century Foundation Task Force on the Future of Unions* (New York: The Century Foundation Press, 1999), (statement of Jay Mazur, David Smith, and Robert Welsh); AFL-CIO estimate, cited in *What's Next for Organized Labor?* 41 (statement of Lewis B. Kaden, Eugene Keilin, Carol O'Clericain, and Bruce Simon).

16. Kate Bronfenbrenner, "No Holds Barred—The Intensification of Employer Opposition to Organizing," Economic Policy Institute, May 20, 2009, 23, http://www.epi.org/publications/entry/bp235.

17. Ibid., 14.

18. Kenneth G. Dau-Scmidt, "The Changing Face of Collective Representation: The Future of Collective Bargaining," *Chicago–Kent Law Review* 82, no. 59 (2007): 916.

19. Roger C. Hartley, "Non-Legislative Labor Law Reform and Pre-Recognition Labor Neutrality Agreements: The Newest Civil Rights Movement," *Berkeley Journal of Employee and Labor Law* 22 (2001): 369.

20. *Seventy-Fourth Annual Report of the National Labor Relations Board Year Ended September 30, 2009* (Washington, D.C.: National Labor Relations Board, February 23, 2w.nlrb.gov/sites/default/files/documents/119/nlrb2009.pdf.

21. Bronfenbrenner, "No Holds Barred," 8.

22. Ibid., 7–8.

23. Ibid., 8.

24. See chapter 5.

25. Bronfenbrenner, "No Holds Barred," 24.

26. Ibid.

27. Marjorie Murphy, *Blackboard Unions: The AFT and the NEA 1900–1980* (Ithaca, N.Y.: Cornell University Press, 1990), 214.

28. Henry S. Farber, "Union Membership in the United States: The Divergence between the Public and Private Sectors," paper presented to the Teacher Collective Bargaining Conference, 2005, 1, http://www.irs.princeton.edu/pubs/pdfs/503.pdf.

29. "Union Members—2010," Bureau of Labor Statistics, January 21, 2011, http://www.bls.gov/news.release/union2.nr0.htm.

30. Steven Greenhouse, "Most Union Members Are Working for the Government, New Data Shows," *New York Times*, January 23, 2010.

31. Barry T. Hirsch, "Unions, Dynamism, and Economic Performance," *Research Handbook on the Economics of Labor and Employment Law*, ed. Cynthia L. Estlund and Michael L. Wachter (Northampton, Mass.: Edward Elgar Publishing, 2010), 2, http://www.industrystudies.pitt.edu/pittsburgh11/documents/Papers/PDF%20Papers/3-5%20Hirsch.pdf.

32. Ben Zipperer and John Schmitt, "Union Busting Is Big Business," *The Topeka Capital Journal*, April 6, 2007, http://cjonline.com/stories/070607/opi_182563658.shtml.

33. Geoghegan, *Which Side Are You On?* 268.

34. Ronald L. Seeber and William N. Cooke, "The Decline in Union Success in NLRB Representation Elections," *Industrial Relations* 22, no. 1 (1983): 34–44, 42.

35. John-Paul Ferguson, "The Eyes of the Needles: A Sequential Model of Union Organizing Drives, 1999–2004," *Industrial and Labor Relations Review* 62, no. 1 (2008): 3–21, 11.

36. John J. Lawler, "Testimony of John J. Lawler before the Commission on the Future of Worker-Management Relations," *Federal Documents* 354, 3 (1994), http://digitalcommons.ilr.cornell.edu/cgi/viewcontent.cgi?article=1359&context=key_workplace&sei-redir=1#.

37. William N. Cooke, "Determinants of the Outcomes of Union Certification Elections," *Industrial and Labor Relations Review* 36, no. 3 (1983): 402–14, 406.

38. "2008 Annual Survey of Violations of Trade Union Rights—USA," International Trade Union Confederation, November 20, 2008, http://www.unhcr.org/refworld/docid/4c52ca6423.html.

39. Kate Bronfenbrenner and Robert Hickey, "Changing to Organize: A National Assessment of Union Organizing Strategies," Articles and Chapters paper 54, 2004, 17–55, Table 1.4, http://digitalcommons.ilr.cornell.edu/articles/54.

40. John Logan, "U.S. Anti-Union Consultants: A Threat to the Rights of British Workers," Trade Union Congress, www.tuc.org.uk/extras/loganreport.pdf.

41. See chapter 5.

42. *Seventy-Fourth Annual Report of the National Labor Relations Board*, Table 23, www.nlrb.gov/sites/default/files/documents/119/nlrb2009.pdf.

43. Ibid. The NLRB does not separate out the time it takes to resolve unlawful discharges from other unfair labor practices.

44. Ibid., table 4.

45. Lafe E. Solomon, "Guideline Memorandum Regarding Backpay Mitigation," NLRB Office of the General Counsel, 2, mynlrb.nlrb.gov/link/document.aspx/09031d458045d137.

46. If she is an undocumented worker, she would not be eligible for backpay, even if she found no comparable employment. *Hoffman Plastic Compounds, Inc. v. NLRB*, 535 U.S. 137 (2002).

47. Geoghegan, *Which side Are You On?* 254.

48. Ibid.

49. William H. Holley, Kenneth M. Jennings, and Roger S. Wolters, *The Labor Relations Process*, 9th ed. (Mason, Ohio: South-Western Cengage Learning, 2009), 96.

50. James Ellis Davis, "The Exclusive Jurisdiction of the NLRB as a Limitation on the Application of RICO to Labor Disputes," *Kentucky Law Journal* 76 (1987): 201–36, 201–02.

51. Garrett Keizer, "Public or Private, It's Work," *New York Times,* June 24, 2011, http://www.nytimes.com/2011/06/25/opinion/25keizer.html.

52. Memorandum from David L. Christlieb of Littler Mendelson to supervisors at Dart, June 28, 2004,www.unionbusting101.com/Top_Secret.pdf.

53. "Union Members—2010," table 2.

54. Ibid., table 3.

55. "Employee Benefits in the United States," Bureau of Labor Statistics, tables 1–4, www.bls.gov/ncs/ebs/sp/ebnr0016.pdf; Lawrence Mishel and Matthew Walter, "How Unions Help All Workers," Economic Policy Institute, 2003, table 4, http://www.epi.org/page/-/old/briefingpapers/143/bp143.pdf.

56. John W. Budd, "The Effect of Unions on Employee Benefits: Updated Employer Expenditure Results," *Journal of Labor Research* 26, no. 4 (2005): 669–76.

57. For a recent example, see Thomas Geoghegan, "Boeing's Threat to American Enterprise," *Wall Street Journal,* June 20, 2011.

58. Geoghegan, *Which Side Are You On?* 254–55.

59. "Obstacles to Organizing under the Railway Labor Act," American Rights at Work, www.americanrightsatwork.org/publications/general/obstacles-to-organizing-under-the-railway-labor-act.html.

60. "Railroaded Out of Their Rights: How a Labor Law Loophole Prevents FedEx Express Employees from Being Represented by a Union," The Leadership Conference on Civil and Human Rights, 7, http://www.civilrights.org/publications/fedex-rla-loophole/; and Rafael Gelyal, "A Tale of Three Statutes . . . (and One Industry); A Case Study on the Competitive Effects of Regulation," *Oregon Law Review* 80 (2001): 947–1005, 986.

61. "Obstacles to Organizing under the Railway Labor Act."

62. Charles J. Morris, "A Tale of Two Statutes: Discrimination for Union Activity under the NLRA and RLA," *Employee Rights and Employment Policy Journal* 2, no. 317 (1998): 3.

63. Gelyal, "A Tale of Three Statutes," 986–87.

64. Morris, 7–8.

Chapter Four

1. Peter Bailey, "History of Human Rights," Universal Rights Network, http://www.universalrights.net/main/creation.htm.

2. Christian Tomuschat, "International Covenant on Civil and Political Rights," United Nations Treaty Collection, http://untreaty.un.org/cod/avl/ha/iccpr/iccpr.html.

3. Richard D. Kahlenberg, *Tough Liberal: Albert Shanker and the Battles Over Schools, Unions, Race and Democracy* (New York: Columbia University Press, 2007), 253; "Al Shanker, Tough Liberal," transcript, PBS *Think Tank,* http://www.pbs.org/thinktank/transcript1284.html.

4. Preamble of The Universal Declaration of Human Rights, http://www.un.org/en/documents/udhr/index.shtml (accessed 11/25/2011).

5. Peter G. Danchin, "The Universal Declaration of Human Rights," Columbia Center for New Media Teaching and Learning, http://ccnmtl.columbia.edu/projects/mmt/udhr/index.html.

6. "American Declaration of the Rights and Duties of Man," University of Minnesota Human Rights Library, http://www1.umn.edu/humanrts/oasinstr/zoas2dec.htm.

7. Tomuschat, "International Covenant on Civil and Political Rights."

8. "International Covenant on Economic, Social and Cultural Rights," Office of the United Nations High Commissioner for Human Rights, http://www2.ohchr.org/english/law/cescr.htm.

9. Tomuschat, "International Covenant on Civil and Political Rights."

10. "International Covenant on Civil and Political Rights."

11. "American Convention on Human Rights," Human and Constitutional Rights Resource Page, http://www.hrcr.org/docs/American_Convention/oashr5.html.

12. "What Is the IACHR?" Inter-American Commission on Human Rights, http://www.cidh.oas.org/what.htm.

13. Nadia Ezzelarab and Brian Tittemore, "Round Table Discusses U.S. Ratification of Inter-American Convention on Human Rights," The Human Rights Brief, http://www.wcl.american.edu/hrbrief/v2i1/iaconv21.htm.

14. *OECD Guidelines for Multinational Enterprises* (Paris: Organisation for Economic Co-operation and Development, 2008), 17, http://www.oecd.org/dataoecd/56/36/1922428.pdf.

15. Kimberly Ann Elliott and Richard B. Freeman, "The ILO to the Rescue?" in *Can Labor Standards Improve Under Globalization?* (Washington, D.C.: Institute for International Economics, 2003), 94.

16. Ibid.

17. Eric Gravel, Isabelle Duplessis, and Bernard Gernigon, *The Committee on Freedom of Association: Its Impact over 50 Years* (Geneva: International Labour Office, 2002), 7.

18. Ibid.

19. Elliot and Freeman, "The ILO to the Rescue?" 95.

20. Ibid., 108.

21. "Fundamental International Labour Standards on Freedom of Association," International Labour Organization, http://ilo-mirror.library.cornell.edu/public/english/standards/norm/whatare/fundam/foa.htm.

22. "Convention No. C087," International Labour Organization, IOLEX—Database of International Labor Standards, http://www.ilo.org/ilolex/cgi-lex/ratifce.pl?C087.

23. "Convention No. C098," International Labour Organization, IOLEX—Database of International Labor Standards, http://www.ilo.org/ilolex/cgi-lex/ratifce.pl?C098 (providing a full list of countries that are signatories to the convention).

24. "Fundamental International Labour Standards on Freedom of Association"

25. Ibid.

26. Nancy H. Chau and S. M. Ravi Kanbur, "The Adoption of International Labor Standards Conventions: Who, When, and Why?" *Brookings Trade Forum* (Washington, D.C.: Brookings Institution, 2001), 151, http://www.arts.cornell.edu/poverty/kanbur/ckbrookings07-03.pdf.

27. "ILO 'Core' Conventions Ratifications Surge past 1,000 Mark," press release, International Labour Organization, http://www.ilo.org/global/about-the-ilo/press-and-media-centre/press-releases/WCMS_007909/lang--en/index.htm.

28. Elliott and Freeman, "The ILO to the Rescue?" 107. Curiously, though America has refused to sign the ILO Conventions on workers' rights, it was a signatory to the Inter-American Democratic Charter in 2001. Article 10 of the Charter affirms the

importance of the ILO labor standards, stating: "The promotion and strengthening of democracy requires the full and effective exercise of workers' rights and the application of core labor standards, as recognized in the International Labour Organization (ILO) Declaration on Fundamental Principles and Rights at Work, and its Follow-up, adopted in 1998, as well as other related fundamental ILO conventions. Democracy is strengthened by improving standards in the workplace and enhancing the quality of life for workers in the Hemisphere." "Inter-American Democratic Charter," Organization of American States, September 11, 2001, http://www.oas.org/en/democratic-charter/pdf/demcharter_en.pdf#page=10.

29. North Carolina General Statute § 95-98.

30. ILO, GB.298/7/1, 298th Session, 948 (March 2007).

31. Ibid, 999.

32. Letter from Robert B. Shepard, Office of International Relations, U.S. Department of Justice, to Victoria Voight, Special Deputy Attorney General, North Carolina Department of Justice, July 31, 2007, on file with authors.

33. Arch Puddington, "The Global State of Workers' Rights—Free Labor in a Hostile World," Freedom House, August 2010, www.freedomhouse.org/uploads/special_report/92.pdf.

34. Ibid.

35. Ibid., 53.

36. Ibid., 51.

37. Ibid., 3.

38. Ibid., 9.

39. Ibid., 53.

40. Ibid., 24.

41. Thomas Geoghegan, *Were You Born on the Wrong Continent? How the European Model Can Help You Get a Life* (New York: Basic Books, 2010), 113.

42. Ibid., 113–17.

43. Ibid., 113 and 227.

44. "The Global State of Workers' Rights," 23.

45. Ibid., 23.

46. John Logan, "Union Recognition and Collective Bargaining: How Does the United States Compare with Other Democracies?" in *Academics on Employee Free Choice* (Berkeley: University of California–Berkeley Center for Labor Research and Education, 2009), 47.

47. John Schmitt and Alexandra Mitukiewicz, "Politics Matter: Changes in Unionization Rates in Rich Countries, 1960–2010," Center for Economic and Policy Research, November 2011, 5, http://www.cepr.net/index.php/publications/reports/changes-in-unionization-rates-in-rich-countries-1960-2010.

48. Puddington, "The Global State of Workers' Rights," 45.

49. Ibid., 45.

50. Ibid., 51–53.

51. Lance A. Compa, *Unfair Advantage: Workers' Freedom of Association in the United States Under International Human Rights Standards* (New York: Human Rights Watch, 2000), 307.

52. Lance A. Compa, *A Strange Case: Violations of Workers' Freedom of Association in the United States by European Multinational Corporations* (New York: Human Rights Watch, 2010), 15.

53. Logan, "Union Recognition and Collective Bargaining," 48.

54. Theodore J. St. Antoine, "Federal Regulation of the Workplace in the Next Half Century," *Chicago-Kent Law Review* 61 (1985): 639, http://heinonline.org/HOL/Page?collection=journals&handle=hein.journals /chknt61&id=643.

55. Ibid.

56. Logan, "Union Recognition and Collective Bargaining," 47.

57. Puddington, "The Global State of Workers' Rights," 9.

58. Logan, "Union Recognition and Collective Bargaining," 48.

59. Puddington, "The Global State of Workers' Rights," 46.

60. Ibid., 10.

Chapter Five

1. It should be noted, however, that both federal labor and employment laws were passed pursuant to the Commerce Clause. See Proceeding *N.L.R.B. v. Jones & Laughlin Steel Corp.*, 301 U.S. 1 (1937); 42 U.S.C. §2000-e(b), (d), (e). There is an interesting history, however, to the struggle to get the NLRA passed pursuant to the Thirteenth Amendment, which bans slavery, by using the argument that, without full protections to join a union and bargain collectively, the employee is effectively an involuntary servant. See James Gray Pope, "The Thirteenth Amendment Versus the Commerce Clause: Labor and the Shaping of American Constitutional Law, 1921–1957," *Columbia Law Review* 102, no. 1 (2002): 46–59.

2. Currently only Montana has a for-cause system for private sector employees. In Montana, as a statutory right, an employee in the private sector may not be terminated without "good cause." MONT. CODE ANN. § 39-2-903(5) (2007).

3. *Engquist v. Oregon Dept. of Agriculture,* 128 S.Ct. 2146, 2155-56 (2008). *See* 82 Am. Jur. 2d Wrongful Discharge §1, n. 4, for dozens of cases from a variety of circuits that use this formulation, including the common "good cause, bad cause, or no cause" formulation.

4. Public sector employees have the additional protections of state and federal civil service laws.

5. 45 U.S.C. §152.

6. 29 U.S.C. §157.

7. In addition to the protections offered by Title VII, a variety of statutes contain protections against retaliation for whistleblowers. See Moshe Marvit, "The Engquist Revolution: How the Supreme Court Affirmed Arbitrary Action in Public Employment," *William and Mary Policy Review* 1 (2010): 142–43 .

8. 42 U.S.C. §2000e-2.

9. Age Discrimination in Employment Act of 1967, Pub. L. 90-202 (1967), codified at 29 U.S.C.A. §§ 621 et seq.

10. Pregnancy Discrimination Act of 1978, Pub. L. 95-555 (1978), codified at 42 U.S.C. § 2000e(k).

11. Americans with Disabilities Act of 1990, Pub. L. 101-336 (1990), codified at 42 U.S.C.A. §§ 12101 et seq.

12. Uniform Services Employment and Reemployment Rights Act of 1994, 38 U.S.C. §4311.

13. Genetic Information Nondiscrimination Act of 2008, Pub. L. 110-233 (2008).

14. 11 U.S.C. §525.

15. See e.g. N.Y. Exec. Law § 296 (McKinney).

16. See e.g. Cal. Gov't Code § 12940 (West).

17. Wis. Stat. Ann. § 111.31 (West).

18. Wash. Rev. Code Ann. § 49.60.180 (West).

19. Or. Rev. Stat. Ann. § 659.785 (West).

20. *P. Gas and Elec. Co. v. State Energy Resources Conservation & Dev. Commn.,* 461 U.S. 190, 203-04 (1983) (citations omitted) ("It is well-established that within Constitutional limits Congress may preempt state authority by so stating in express terms. Absent explicit preemptive language, Congress' intent to supersede state law altogether may be found from a 'scheme of federal regulation so pervasive as to make reasonable the inference that Congress left no room to supplement it,' 'because the Act of Congress may touch a field in which the federal interest is so dominant that the federal system will be assumed to preclude enforcement of state laws on the same subject,' or because "the object sought to be obtained by the federal law and the character of obligations imposed by it may reveal the same purpose.' Even where Congress has not entirely displaced state regulation in a specific area, state law is preempted to the extent that it actually conflicts with federal law. Such a conflict arises when 'compliance with both federal and state regulations is a physical impossibility,' or where state law 'stands as an obstacle to the accomplishment and execution of the full purposes and objectives of Congress.'")

21. See e.g. *AT&T Mobility LLC v. Concepcion,* 131 S. Ct. 1740 (2011).

22. Steven Greenhouse, "Strained States Turning to Laws to Curb Labor Unions," *New York Times,* January 3, 2011.

23. 42 U.S.C. § 2000e-2(a)(1).

24. 29 U.S.C. §157.

25. See generally NLRB Rules and Regulations and Statement of Procedure, http://www.nlrb.gov/sites/default/files/documents/254/rulesregsfull.pdf.

26. Ibid.., §101.8.

27. Ibid., §101.6.

28. See *San Diego Bldg. Trades Council v. Garmon,* 353 U.S. 26, 77 S. Ct. 607, 1 L. Ed. 2d 618 (1957), for the Supreme Court's original statement on NLRA preemption of state law. See Benjamin I. Sachs, "Employment Law as Labor Law," *Cardozo Law Review* 29 (2008): 2685, for alternate routes to relief not based on the NLRA or state law.

29. Ibid., §101.10.

30. NLRB Casehandling Manual, Part 1: Unfair Labor Practice Proceedings, §10292.4, http://www.nlrb.gov/sites/default/files/documents/44/chm_ulp_2011.pdf. See also *NLRB v. Robbins Tire & Rubber Co.,* 437 U.S. 214 (1978).

31. Fed. R. Civ. P. 26(b)(1).

32. NLRB Rules and Regulations and Statement of Procedure, at §101.11(b).

33. See Wilma B. Liebman, "Decline and Disenchantment: Reflections on the Aging of the National Labor Relations Board," *Berkeley Journal of Employment and Labor Law* 28 (2007): 578; James J. Brudney, "A Famous Victory: Collective Bargaining Protections and the Statutory Aging Process," *North Carolina Law Review* 74 (1996): 939.

34. See *Livadas v. Bradshaw,* 512 U.S. 107 (1994).

35. *Seventy-Fourth Annual Report of the National Labor Relations Board for the Fiscal Year Ended September 30, 2009* (Washington, D.C.: National Labor Relations Board, February 23, 2010).

36. 42 U.S.C. §2000e-9.

37. *Fiscal Year 2010 Performance and Accountability Report,* United States Equal Employment Opportunity Commission, 32.

38. 42 U.S.C. §2000e-5(f)(1).

39. See e.g. *Weber v. Holiday Inn,* 42 F. Supp. 2d 693, 698 (E.D. Tex. 1999).

40. *Weir v. Potter,* 214 F. Supp. 2d 53, 55 (D. Mass. 2002).

41. 42 U.S.C. §2000e-5(f)(1).

42. 42 U.S.C. §2000e-5(k).

43. See *Alyeska Pipeline Serv. Co. v. Wilderness Society,* 421 U.S. 240 (1975), for a discussion on the "American Rule."

44. *Franks v. Bowman Transportation Co.,* 424 U.S. 747, 764 (1976).

45. 42 U.S.C. §1981a.

46. Backpay awards under the NLRA and Title VII are significantly similar. See NLRB Casehandling Manual, Part III, §10544.

47. 42 U.S.C. §2000c-5(g)(2)(B).

48. *Gaworski v. ITT Commercial Finance Corp.,* 17 F.3d 1104 (8th Cir. 1994).

49. *Ford Motor Co. v. EEOC,* 458 U.S. 219 (1982).

50. *Thorne v. City of El Segundo,* 802 F.2d 1131 (9th Cir. 1986).

51. *Robinson v. Metro-N. Commuter R.R. Co.,* 267 F.3d 147 (2d Cir. 2001).

52. 42 U.S.C. §1981.

53. 42 U.S.C.A. § 1981a(b)(3); EEOC Policy Guide, 405: 7096-97.

54. 42 U.S.C. §1981a(b)(1).

55. 42 U.S.C. §1981a(b)(3).

56. Civil Rights Act of 1991, § 103(c)(1).

57. Jean R. Sternlight, "In Search of the Best Procedure for Enforcing Employment Discrimination Laws: A Comparative Analysis," *Tulane Law Review* 78 (2004): 1423.

58. "ADR Vision Roundtable: Challenge for the 21st Century," *Dispute Resolution Journal* 56 (October 2001): 8.

59. Fed. R. Civ. P. 26.

60. See John R. Dunne, "Civil Rights in the 1990's," *Hofstra Labor Law Journal* 9 (1992): 289.

61. Thomas Geoghegan, *Which Side Are You On? Trying to Be for Labor When It's Flat on Its Back* (New York: Farrar, Straus and Giroux, 1991), 267.

62. Sachs, "Employment Law as Labor Law," 2715–21.

63. Ibid., 2715–17.

64. Ibid., 2718.

65. 29 U.S.C. 158(a)(1); 29 U.S.C. 158(a)(3).

66. Sachs, "Employment Law as Labor Law," 2719–20.

67. *In Re Ishikawa Gasket Am., Inc.,* 337 NLRB 175, 177 (N.L.R.B. 2001).

68. *J & R Flooring, Inc. d/b/a J. Picini Flooring and Freemans Carpet Serv., Inc. and Fcs Flooring, Inc. Flooring Solutions of Nevada, Inc., d/b/a Fsi and Intl. Union of Painters and Allied Trades, Dist. Council 15.,* 356 NLRB No. 9 (N.L.R.B. Oct. 22, 2010).

69. Sachs, "Employment Law as Labor Law," 2721.

70. Ibid.

71. 79 Cong. Rec. 10720 (1935) (statement of President Franklin D. Roosevelt on signing the National Labor Relations Act (the Wagner Act), on July 5, 1935); Legislative History of the National Labor Relations Act 3269 (1935).

72. Sachs, "Employment Law as Labor Law," 2690–92.

73. One could make the argument that the seeds of failure were planted in the NLRA with the passage of Taft-Hartley in 1947. Not only did Taft-Hartley make

major changes to the NLRA, such as prohibiting secondary boycotts, closed shops, and "unfair labor practices" by unions, it also prohibited the NLRB from employing economic analysts. 29 U.S.C. §154(a). Chairwoman Liebman has stated that "[This provision] makes the Board ill-equipped to modernize labor law doctrines in response to a changing economy, let alone to make informed decisions based on economic realities. By design or happenstance, this handicap effectively promotes the Board's obsolescence." Liebman, "Decline and Disenchantment," 578. With the NLRB unable to adapt labor law to modern circumstances, some have found empirical evidence that the apellate courts have been engaged in an effort to reshape the NLRA to fit changing external norms. Brudney, "A Famous Victory."

74. The Failure of Labor Law—A Betrayal of American Workers, Report of Sub-comm. on Labor-Management Relations, House Comm. on Educ. & Lab., 98th Cong. (1984).

75. Paul Weiler, "Promises to Keep: Securing Workers' Rights to Self-Organization under the NLRA," *Harvard Law Review* 96 (1983): 1769.

76. Katherine V. W. Stone, *From Widgets to Digits: Employment Regulation for the Changing Workplace* (New York: Cambridge University Press, 2004); Cynthia L. Estlund, "The Ossification of American Labor Law," *Columbia Law Review* 102 (2002): 1527.

77. Liebman, "Decline and Disenchantment," 570–71.

78. See e.g. Charles B. Craver, "The National Labor Relations Act Must Be Revised to Preserve Industrial Democracy," *Arizona Law Review* 34 (1992): 397.

79. See chapter 7,

80. See e.g. Michael H. Gottesman, "In Despair, Starting over: Imagining A Labor Law for Unorganized Workers," *Chicago-Kent Law Review* 69 (1993): 59.

81. For example, the AFL-CIO lists some of the corporate and anti-union groups that have spent tens of millions of dollars to defeat EFCA, http://www.aflcio.org/joinaunion/voiceatwork/efca/against_list.cfm#_edn7.

82. Sachs, "Employment Law as Labor Law," 2687.

83. Ibid.

84. Ibid., 2690–92.

85. Liebman, "Decline and Disenchantment," 573.

86. Thomas Geoghegan, "Boeing's Threat to American Enterprise," *Wall Street Journal,* June 20, 2011.

87. Liebman, "Decline and Disenchantment," 572.

88. Much of this model statute was informed by discussions and a model statute drafted by the labor attorney and author, Thomas Geoghegan.

89. For a discussion on how the individual rights model can diminish collective rights, see Nelson Lichtenstein, *State of the Union: A Century of American Labor* (Princeton, N.J.: Princeton University Press, 2002).

90. *Palace Sports & Ent., Inc. v. N.L.R.B.,* 411 F.3d 212, 220 (D.C. Cir. 2005).

91. *N. L. R. B. v. Burnup & Sims, Inc.,* 379 U.S. 21, 23 (1964).

92. See discussion in chapter 3, 43–44.

93. Ellen Dannin, *Taking Back the Workers' Law: How to Fight the Assault on Labor Rights* (Cornell, N.Y.: Cornell University Press, 2006).

94. See e.g. *Hardrick v. Airway Freight Sys., Inc.,* 98 C 1609, 2000 WL 263687 (N.D. Ill. Feb. 28, 2000); *Talbott v. Empress River Casino,* 95 C 5317, 1997 WL 458437 (N.D. Ill. Aug. 4, 1997).

95. *Barrow v. Falck,* 977 F.2d 1100, 1105 (7th Cir. 1992).

96. Ibid.

97. *Ford Motor Co. v. EEOC,* 458 U.S. 219 (1982).

98. 29 U.S.C. §152(2), (3).

99. H.R. 8677, 93d Cong., 1st Sess., 119 CONG. REC. 19,271 (1973). This failed bill would have amended the NLRA definition of "employer" to include state and local government employees.

100. Compare 29 U.S.C. § 152 to 42 U.S.C. § 2000e.

101. 29 U.S.C. § 151.

102. Michael H. LeRoy and Wallace Hendricks, "Should 'Agricultural Laborers' Continue to Be Excluded from the National Labor Relations Act?" *Emory Law Journal* 48 (1999): 505.

103. Juan F. Perea, "The Echoes of Slavery: Recognizing the Racist Origins of the Agricultural and Domestic Worker Exclusion from the National Labor Relations Act," *Ohio State Law Journal* 72 (2011): 95.

104. Social Security Act of 1935, c. 531, 49 Stat. 620 (codified in scattered sections of 42 U.S.C.).

105. Perea, "The Echoes of Slavery."

106. "Agricultural Safety," Centers for Disease Control and Prevention, National Institute for Occupational Safety and Health, http://www.cdc.gov/niosh/topics/aginjury/.

107. "Farm Safety," OSHA Fact Sheet, Occupational Health and Safety Administration, 2002, http://www.nmsu.edu/safety/resources/forms/OSHA-FarmHealth& Safetyfacts2.pdf.

108. "A Report on the Conditions of Migrant and Seasonal Farmworkers in Michigan," Michigan Civil Rights Commission, March, 2010, 42.

109. "Agricultural Safety."

110. Bon Appetit Management Company and United Farm Workers, "Inventory of Farmworker Issues and Protections in the United States," 10, http://bamco.com/ sustainable-food-service/farmworker-inventory.

111. "A Report on the Conditions of Migrant and Seasonal Farmworkers in Michigan."

112. Ibid., 10–15.

113. Ibid., 38–42.

114. Ibid., 34–38.

115. 29 U.S.C. 213(a)(6).

116. Several states, particularly on the west coast have enacted state level minimum wage and overtime protections.

117. "The Erlenborn Commission Report," *Georgia Immigration Law Journal* 15 (2000): 115.

118. Labor Management Relations Act, 1947 (Taft-Hartley Act), Pub. L. 80-101, 61 Stat. 136 (codified as amended at 29 U.S.C. §§ 141-197).

119. 330 U.S. 485 (1947).

120. Ibid., 487–88.

121. Ibid., 494 (J. Douglas dissenting).

122. Ibid.

123. See 29 U.S.C. §151.

124. *Packard Motor Car Co. (Detroit, Mich.),* 61 NLRB 4 , 33 (Reilly, dissenting) (1945).

125. 330 U.S. at 490.

126. H.R.Rep. No. 245 at 16 and 17, 80th Cong., 1st Sess. 4, reprinted in 1 NLRB, Legislative History of the Labor Management Relations Act, 1947 at 307 to 308.

127. H.R.Rep. No. 245 at 13 and 14, 80th Cong., 1st Sess. 4, reprinted in I NLRB, Legislative History of the Labor Management Relations Act, 1947 at 304 to 305.

128. 29 U.S.C. §152(11).

129. See *Jochims v. National Labor Relations Bd.*, 480 F.3d 1161 (D.C. Cir. 2007); *Public Service Co. of Colorado v. N.L.R.B.*, 405 F.3d 1071 (10th Cir. 2005); *Hospital General Menonita v. N.L.R.B.*, 393 F.3d 263 (1st Cir. 2004).

130. 29 U.S.C. §152(12); see David M. Rabban, "Distinguishing Excluded Managers from Covered Professionals under the NLRA," *Columbia Law Review* 89 (1989): 1776, for a discussion on the tension between the NLRB's definition for supervisor and professional. *See also* Marion Crain, "The Transformation of the Professional Workforce," *Chicago-Kent Law Review* 79 (2004): 611, for a discussion on how the commodification of professionals indicates that they no longer fit the definition of having "independent judgment."

131. See the *Kentucky River Trilogy: Oakwood Healthcare, Inc.*, 348 NLRB No. 37 (September 29, 2006); *Golden Crest Healthcare Center*, 348 NLRB No. 39 (September 29, 2006); and *Croft Metals, Inc.*, 348 NLRB No. 38 (September 29, 2006).

132. *In Re Oakwood Healthcare, Inc.*, 348 NLRB 686 (N.L.R.B. 2006) (Liebman and Walsh dissenting in part, concurring in the result).

133. John Hensley and Debra D. Burke, "The Changing Nature of Supervision: Implications for Labor-Management Relations in the Twenty-First Century," *Seton Hall Legislative Journal* 33 (2009): 427.

134. It should be noted that the NLRA explicitly allows employers to recognize a supervisor union. 29 U.S.C.A. § 164(a). ("Nothing herein shall prohibit any individual employed as a supervisor from becoming or remaining a member of a labor organization, but no employer subject to this subchapter shall be compelled to deem individuals defined herein as supervisors as employees for the purpose of any law, either national or local, relating to collective bargaining.")

135. 29 U.S.C. § 152(2).

136. *Hutchinson v. Magee*, 122 A. 234, 234 (Pa. 1923).

137. *City of Springfield v. Clouse*, 206 S.W.2d 539, 545 (Mo. 1947) (citations omitted) overruled by *Indep.-Nat. Educ. Ass'n v. Indep. Sch. Dist.*, 223 S.W.3d 131 (Mo. 2007). ("It is a familiar principal of constitutional law that the legislature cannot delegate its legislative powers and any attempted delegation thereof is void. If such powers cannot be delegated, they surely cannot be bargained or contracted away.")

138. Clyde W. Summers, "Public Sector Bargaining: Problems of Governmental Decisionmaking," *University of Cincinnati Law Review* (1975): 674. The "two bites at the apple" concern posits that public sector employees will have both the access of the citizen in the public sphere, and then will also have a special private access of the collective bargaining process. The concern is that a public sector union negotiating the terms and conditions of public employment will necessarily affect policy, creating a special avenue of access to a special interest with regards to public policy.

Contrasting private and public sector unions in the late 1960s, Professors Harry H. Wellington and Ralph K. Winter counseled against implementing a private sector form of labor law in the public sector because the private market forces that keep private sector unions in place will not have a similar effect on public sector unions:

In the private sector, a high degree of substitutability between various products generally exists: a price increase of one product relative to others will result in a decrease in the number of units of that product sold as consumers adjust their preferences to changed price relationships. Wage increases which exceed rises in productivity usually result in higher prices. Private sector unions generally face, therefore, a trade-off between the level of benefits they can extract from an employer and the level of employment for union members they can maintain. . . .

In the public sector, the trade-off between increased benefits and employment is of little importance to public employee unions. The products and services provided by government generally do not have close substitutes and are not subject to competition from non-union enterprises. The reduction of unionized governmental services, more-over, will be resisted not only by the union involved but also by the beneficiaries of those services-the local voters. The pressure on the political leaders, then, will be either to seek new funds or to reduce other governmental services or subsidies. Harry H. Wellington and Ralph K. Winter, "Structuring Collective Bargaining in Public Employ-ment," *Yale Law Journal* 79 (1970): 807. Wellington and Winter were truly concerned about the distorting the democratic process if public unions could form, strike, and engage in other job actions. They feared that the union would effectively be able to drown out any competing voice. Ibid., 808. However, with the increased privatization of many government services in the past few decades, the authors' fear that public unions would have special strength derived from a monopoly of services is unfounded.

139. See e.g. Yuval Levin, "Collective Bargaining in the Public Sector," *National Review* Online, February 21, 2011, http://www.nationalreview.com/corner/260241/collective-bargaining-public-sector-yuval-levin#.

140. Katherine Van Wezel Stone, "The Post-War Paradigm in American Labor Law," *Yale Law Journal* 90 (1981): 1509.

141. Reuel E. Schiller, "From Group Rights to Individual Liberties: Post-War Labor Law, Liberalism, and the Waning of Union Strength," *Berkeley Journal of Employment and Labor Law* 20 (1999): 6.

142. Ibid., 7.

143. *Communications Workers of Am. v. Beck,* 487 U.S. 735, 745 (1988).

144. *Penrod v. N.L.R.B.,* 203 F.3d 41, 44 (D.C. Cir. 2000).

145. *Abood v. Detroit Bd. of Ed.,* 431 U.S. 209, 221-23 (1977) (citations omitted). Though *Abood* arose in the public sector employment context, the balance remains relevant.

146. 29 U.S.C. § 164(b).

147. See e.g. Ala. Code 1975 § 25-7-30, et. seq.

148. "Table of State Right-to-work Laws as of January 1, 2009," United States Department of Labor, December 2008, http://www.dol.gov/whd/state/righttowork.htm.

149. Steven E. Abraham, "How the Taft-Hartley Act Hindered Unions," *Hofstra Labor Law Journal* 12 (1994): 30.

150. David Kelly, "Do Right-To-Work Laws Protect Workers' Rights?" *Employment Alert* 19 no. 1 (January 3, 2002): 5.

151. 29 U.S.C. § 159.

Chapter Six

1. Alexis de Tocqueville, *Democracy in America* (1835–1840), Chapter 12.

2. *NAACP v. Alabama,* ex rel. Patterson, Attorney General, 357 U.S. 449, 460 (1958).

3. *NAACP v. Alabama,* 357 U.S., 460-61

4. *Thomas v. Collins, Sherriff,* 323 U.S. 516 (1945)

5. *Smith v. Arkansas State Hwy. Employees Local,* 441 U.S. S. Ct. 463 (1979). In the case itself, the Supreme Court upheld the Constitutionality of the Arkansas State Highway Commission's refusal to listen to grievances filed by a union on behalf of its employees. However, the Court nonetheless reaffirmed that the government cannot interfere with the right of association, including the right of employees to join a union.

6. "Employment discrimination," Legal Information Institute, http://topics.law. cornell.edu/wex/Employment_discrimination (pregnancy covered under the Civil Rights Act).

7. 38 U.S.C. Section 4311.

8. Harvey Sanders, "Bankruptcy Code Protects against Discrimination," Business First, January 9, 2006, citing 11 U.S. C. sec. 525 (b), http://www.bizjournals.com/buffalo/stories/2006/01/09/focus3.html.

9. "Whistleblower Protections," U.S. Department of Labor, http://www.dol.gov/compliance/laws/comp-whistleblower.htm.

10. John Hill, "'Ban the Box' Compromise Seen," *Providence Journal,* March 9, 2011.

11. District of Columbia, Office of Human Rights, Human Rights Act of 1977, http://ohr.dc.gov/ohr/cwp/view,a,3,q,491858,ohrNav,|30953|.asp. See also Subchapter 2, Section 2-1402.11, http://ohr.dc.gov/ohr/frames.asp?doc=/ohr/lib/ohr/pro_acts_of_discrimination.pdf.

12. Robert Pear, "Obama Proposes Protecting Unemployed Against Hiring Bias," *New York Times,* September 27, 2011, A14.

13. Julian Bond, "Is Gay Rights a Civil Rights Issue? A Symposium," *Ebony,* July 2004, http://findarticles.com/p/articles/mi_m1077/is_9_59/ai_n6100475/.

14. *Diaz, Celio v. Pan American World Airways, Inc.,* 442 F.2d 385, 389 (5th Cir. 1971).

15. *Wilson, Gregory R. v. Southwest Airlines Co.,* 517 F. Supp. 292 (Dist. Court, N.D. Texas 1981), n.25.

16. Jervis Anderson, *A. Philip Randolph: A Biographical Portrait* (Berkeley, Calif.: University of California Press, 1986), 288, 302. See also Martin Luther King, Jr., *All Labor Has Dignity,* ed. Michael K. Honey (Boston: Beacon Press, 2011), 31–32.

17. King, *All Labor Has Dignity,* xxx, 33; and King, address to AFL-CIO, December 11, 1961, in ibid., 39–40.

18. King, address to AFL-CIO, pp. xiii and 42. See also King, *All Labor Has Dignity,* 14: "Organized labor has proved to be one of the most powerful forces in removing the blight of segregation and discrimination from our nation. . . . Organized labor is one of the Negro's strongest allies in the struggle for freedom." King repeated the sentiment in an address to the Illinois State AFL-CIO on October 7, 1965, suggesting "The two most dynamic movements that reshaped the nation during the past three decades are the labor and civil rights movements. Our combined strength is potentially enormous." King, *All Labor Has Dignity,* 119.

19. Bayard Rustin, "From Protest to Politics: The Future of the Civil Rights Movement," *Commentary,* February 1965, http://www.commentarymagazine.com/article/from-protest-to-politics-the-future-of-the-civil-rights-movement/.

20. Anderson, *A. Philip Randolph,* 261.

21. King, *All Labor Has Dignity,* xiv-xv, 73.

22. Ibid., 47 (SCLC's first year budget); and xxvi (Randolph support for Montgomery Bus Boycott), 23 (re UAW support for Montgomery Bus Boycott).

23. Taylor E. Dark, *The Unions and the Democrats: An Enduring Alliance,* updated ed. (Ithaca, N.Y.: ILR Press, 2001), 57.

24. King, *All Labor Has Dignity,* 76.

25. King, address to the AFL-CIO, in ibid., 34, 42.

26. See Leadership Conference on Civil and Human Rights, "History of The Leadership Conference on Civil and Human Rights and The Leadership Conference Education Fund," http://www.civilrights.org/about/history.html.

27. King, address to UAW, April 27, 1961, in King, *All Labor Has Dignity,* 28.

28. See King, speech to United Packinghouse Workers Union of America, June 11, 1959, in King, *All Labor Has Dignity,* 20.

29. Tami J. Friedman, "Exploiting the North-South Differential: Corporate Power, Southern Politics, and the Decline of Organized Labor after World War II," *Journal of American History* 95, no. 2 (2008): 330, http://jah.oxfordjournals.org/content/95/2/323.full.pdf.

30. King, *All Labor Has Dignity,* xxii (citing Du Bois's 1944 statement).

31. Friedman, "Exploiting the North-South Differential," 331.

32. See e.g. Elizabeth Tandy Shermer, "Counter-Organizing the Sunbelt: Right-to-Work Campaigns and Anti-Union Conservatism, 1943–1958," *Pacific Historical Review* 78, no. 1 (2009): 85; Michael O'Brien, "W. J. Cash, Hegel, and the South," *Journal of Southern History* 44, no. 3 (1978): 379–98; and Michael Honey, "Operation Dixie: Labor and Civil Rights in the Postwar South," *Mississippi Quarterly* 45, no. 4 (Fall 1992): 443–50, http://www.thefreelibrary.com/Operation+Dixie%3A+labor+and+civil+rights+in+the+Postwar+South.-a013784480.

33. King, address to the United Packinghouse Workers of America, October 2, 1957 in King, *All Labor Has Dignity,* 1 and 19; and King, address to AFL-CIO.

34. King, address to AFL-CIO, 38.

35. See "African-American Education," Encyclopedia of American Education, http://american-education.org/48-african-american-education.html; and "Right to Work States," National Right to Work Legal Defense Foundation, http://www.nrtw.org/rtws.htm. There are twenty-two states in all that have "right to work" laws.

36. "Scope of Bargaining," National Council on Teacher Quality, http://www.nctq.org/tr3/scope/#interactiveMap.

37. "Table 5. Union Affiliation of Employed Wage and Salary Workers by State," U.S. Bureau of Labor Statistics, http://www.bls.gov/news.release/union2.t05.htm.

38. King, address to AFL-CIO, 38.

39. "Union Membership—2010," U.S. Bureau of Labor Statistics, Table 1, http://www.bls.gov/news.release/union2.t01.htm.

40. "Union Representation: A Bride to Economic Security and Equal Opportunity for All Workers," Leadership Conference for Civil and Human Rights, 2009; and see discussion below about the ways in which unions reduce employer discretion and the chance for racial and sex discrimination.

41. Richard B. Freeman and Joel Rogers, *What Workers Want,* updated ed. (Ithaca, N.Y.: ILR Press, 2006), 99, exhibit 4.2.

42. Rustin, "From Protest to Politics."

43. King, address to AFL-CIO, 36–37.

44. King, *All Labor Has Dignity,* xviii and 24; King, address to UAW, 27–28; see also King, address to National Maritime Union, October 23, 1962, in King, *All Labor Has Dignity,* 70 ("Emulating the labor movement, we in the South have embraced

mass actions—boycotts, sit-ins, and more recently, a widespread utilization of the ballots.").

45. "Timeline of 1956," Civil Rights Movement Veterans, http://www.crmvet.org/tim/timhis56.htm.

46. "Anti-Integration," *The Crisis*, June–July 1956, 347. http://books.google.com/books?id=llsEAAAAMBAJ&dq.

47. David Metcalf, Kristine Hansen, and Andy Charlwood, "Unions and the Sword of Justice: Unions and Pay Systems, Pay Inequality, Pay Discrimination and Low Pay," Centre for Economic Performance, 2000, 16, http://eprints.lse.ac.uk/20195/1/Unions_and_the_Sword_of_Justice_Unions_and_Pay_Systems%2C_Pay_Inequality%2C_Pay_Discrimination_and_Low_Pay.pdf.

48. "Union Representation."

49. Ibid.

50. Julius G. Getman, "Changing Role of Courts and the Potential Role of Unions in Overcoming Employment Discrimination," *Tulane Law Review* 64 (1990): 1482.

51. "Union Representation."

52. Ann C. Hodges, "Strategies for Combating Sexual Harassment: The Role of Labor Unions," *Texas Journal of Women and the Law* 15 (2006): 213–14.

53. "Union Representation."

54. Hodges, "Strategies for Combating Sexual Harrassment," 213–14.

55. "Union Representation."

56. Laura Beth Nielsen, Robert L. Nelson, and Nyon Lancaster, "Individual Justice or Collective Legal Mobilization? Employment Discrimination Litigation in the Post–Civil Rights United States," *Journal of Empirical Legal Studies* 7, no. 2 (2010): 190.

57. John S. Heywood, "Race Discrimination and Union Voice," *Industrial Relations* 31, no. 3 (1992): 507.

58. King, *All Labor Has Dignity*, p. xiii.

59. Richard D. Kahlenberg, *The Remedy: Class, Race, and Affirmative Action* (New York: Basic Books, 1996), xxvii, citing Stephen B. Oates, *Let the Trumpet Sound: A Life of Martin Luther King Jr.* (New York: Harper and Row, 1982), 434–35.

60. King, *All Labor Has Dignity*, xxxii.

61. Ibid., xiv.

62. Ibid., xiv.

63. King, AFSME address, March 18, 1968, in King, *All Labor Has Dignity*, 175.

Chapter Seven

1. Taylor E. Dark III, "Prospects for Labor Law Reform," *Perspectives on Work* (Summer 2008/Winter 2009): 24, http://www.lera.uiuc.edu/pubs/perspectives/CompArticles/TDexcerpt.pdf.

2. Dark III, "Prospects for Labor Law Reform," 24; and Jacob S. Hacker and Paul Pierson, *Winner-Take-All Politics: How Washington Made the Rich Richer—and Turned Its Back on the Middle Class* (New York: Simon and Schuster, 2010), 129–30.

3. Dark III, "Prospects for Labor Law Reform," 24.

4. "H.R.1409: Employee Free Choice Act of 2009," OpenCongress, http://www.opencongress.org/bill/111-h1409/.

5. Dark III, "Prospects for Labor Law Reform," 24.

6. Matthew Murray, "Business vs. Unions Now Moves Off the Hill," *Roll Call* (Washington), December 13, 2010.

7. Hacker and Pierson, *Winner-Take-All Politics*, 279.

8. Lydia Saad, "Majority Receptive to Law Making Union Organizing Easier," Gallup, March 17, 2009, http://www.gallup.com/poll/116863/Majority-Receptive-Law-Making-Union-Organizing-Easier.aspx.

9. "Lies and Distortion on the Secret Ballot," American Rights at Work, www.americanrightsatwork.org/employee-free-choice-act/resource-library/lies--distortion-on-the-secret-ballot-20080730-596-84-84.html.

10. Thomas Geoghegan, *Which Side Are You On? Trying to Be for Labor When It's Flat on Its Back* (New York: Farrar, Straus and Giroux, 1991), 7.

11. Ibid., 277.

12. Richard B. Freeman and James L. Medoff, *What Do Unions Do?* (New York: Basic Books, 1984), 204, Table 13-4.

13. Alec MacGillis, "Drifting Right, Lincoln Comes Out Against EFCA," *Washington Post,* April 6, 2009.

14. *Public Opinion and Polling around the World: A Historical Encyclopedia,* vol. 1, ed. John Gray Geer (Santa Barbara, Calif.: ABC-CLIO, 2004), 244–46.

15. Krissah Thompson and Dan Balz, "Rand Paul Comments about Civil Rights Stir Controversy," *Washington Post,* May 21, 2010, A1, http://www.washingtonpost.com/wp-dyn/content/article/2010/05/20/AR2010052003500.html.

16. See generally Julius Getman, *Restoring the Power of Unions: It Takes a Movement* (New Haven, Conn.: Yale University Press, 2010), especially 2 and 229–33.

17. See Paul Weiler, "Promises to Keep: Securing Workers' Right to Self-Organization Under the NLRA," *Harvard Law Review* 96 (1983): 1769 (finding that "a major factor" in the decline of American unions "has been the skyrocketing use of coercive and illegal tactics—discriminatory discharges in particular").

18. Geoghegan, *Which Side Are You On?* 252.

19. John L. Lewis was the president of the United Mine Workers and a founding president of the Congress of Industrial Organizations. Norma Rae Webster was the movie name given to Crystal Lee Sutton, a courageous North Carolina textile worker who stood up for labor rights.

20. See "American Labor in U.S. History Textbooks: How Labor's Story Is Distorted in High School History Textbooks," Albert Shanker Institute, July 2010.

21. "Civil Rights and Race Relations," The Gallup Organization for AARP, January 2004, 28, http://assets.aarp.org/rgcenter/general/civil_rights.pdf.

22. "Bush Calls Education "Civil Rights Issue of Our Time," CNN, January 19, 2002, http://articles.cnn.com/2002-01-19/politics/bush.democrats.radio_1_education-overhaul-education-secretary-rod-paige-bush-and-congressional-republicans?_s=PM: ALLPOLITICS (accessed August 9, 2011); and Helene Cooper, "Obama Takes Aim at Inequality in Education," *New York Times,* April 6, 2011, http://www.nytimes.com/2011/04/07/us/politics/07obama.html.

23. Martin Luther King, Jr., *All Labor Has Dignity,* ed. Michael K. Honey (Boston: Beacon Press, 2011), 42.

24. Sharon Rabin Margalioth, "The Significance of Worker Attitudes: Individualism as a Cause for Labor's Decline," *Hofstra Labor and Employment Law Journal* 16 (1998): 134, http://heinonline.org.

25. "Majorities Reject Banning Defamation of Religion: 20 Nation Poll," World Public Opinion, November 20, 2009, http://www.worldpublicopinion.org/pipa/articles/btjusticehuman_rightsra/647.php?nid=&id=&pnt=647.

26. "Majority of Voters Say Protecting Individual Rights Is Government's Chief Role," Rasmussen Reports, December 22, 2010, http://www.rasmussen reports.com/public_content/politics/general_politics/december_2010/majority_of_voters_say_protecting_individual_rights_is_government_s_chief_role.

27. "Right to Work for Less," AFL-CIO, http://www.aflcio.org/issues/legislativealert/stateissues/work/. See also David Madland, Karla Walter, and Nick Bunker, "Unions Make the Middle Class: Without Unions, the Middle Class Withers," Center for American Progress, April 2011, 7, noting that studies clearly document that "right to work" laws are "associated with decreases in per capita income and decreases in wages and salaries" and citing Lonnie Stevans, "The Effect of Endogenous Right-To-Work Laws on Business and Economic Conditions in the United States: A Multivariate Approach," *Review of Law and Economics* 5, no. 1 (2009).

28. NBC News/Wall Street Journal survey, November 2–5, 2011, in Ruy Teixeira, "The Snapshot: Americans Favor Action on Income Inequality," November 14, 2011, http://www.americanprogress.org/issues/2011/11/snapshot111411.html.

29. New York Times/CBS News Poll, October 19–24, 2011, http://s3.documentcloud.org/documents/259646/the-new-york-times-cbs-news-poll-oct-2011.pdf (also cited in Greg Sargent, "A Nation of Class Warriors," *Washington Post*, October 27, 2011, A21; and Robert Reich, "Income Disparity Matters," *Marketplace*, National Public Radio, November 3, 2011).

30. Gallup Poll, cited in Ed Rogers, "Obama's Misstep on Class Warfare," *Washington Post*, December 15, 2011.

31. Geoghegan, *Which Side Are You On?* 284.

32. Thomas Geoghegan, *Were You Born on the Wrong Continent? How the European Model Can Help You Get a Life* (New York: New Press, 2010), 288. In other ways, the creation of a private right of action for discrimination on the basis of union membership may prove a cost saver for the government because cases that might have otherwise stagnated at the NLRB for three years or more on the government's dime, would now be able to be taken over by the aggrieved worker.

33. *New York Times*/CBS News Poll, October 19–24, 2011, finding that 28 percent say the policies of the Obama administration "favor the rich" compared with 23 percent saying they "favor the middle class," 17 percent "favor the poor," and 21 percent "treat all groups equally." See also Michael Tomasky, "Rich Man Rules," *The Daily Beast*, October 26, 2011.

34. "Polling On Unions," National Journal Poll Track, 2005, http://www3.national journal.com/members/polltrack/2005/national/05unions.htm.

35. Richard B. Freeman, "Do Workers Till Want Unions? More Than Ever," Economic Policy Institute, February 22, 2007, 6–7.

36. Mark Murray, "NBC/WSJ Poll: 62 percent against Stripping Public Employees' Bargaining Rights," MSNBC, March 2, 2011, http://firstread.msnbc.msn.com/_news/2011/03/02/6171265-nbcwsj-poll-62-against-stripping-public-employees-bargaining-rights.

37. Sabrina Tavernise and Steven Greenhouse, "Ohio Vote on Labor Is Parsed for Omens," *New York Times*, November 9, 2011.

Index

About the Authors

RICHARD D. KAHLENBERG is a senior fellow at The Century Foundation. He is the author of four books: *Tough Liberal: Albert Shanker and the Battles Over Schools, Unions, Race and Democracy* (Columbia University Press, 2007); *All Together Now: Creating Middle-Class Schools through Public School Choice* (Brookings Institution Press, 2001); *The Remedy: Class, Race, and Affirmative Action* (Basic Books, 1996); and *Broken Contract: A Memoir of Harvard Law School* (Hill & Wang/ Farrar, Straus & Giroux, 1992). In addition, Kahlenberg is the editor of eight Century Foundation books: *The Future of School Integration: Socioeconomic Diversity as an Education Reform Strategy* (2012); *Affirmative Action for the Rich: Legacy Preferences in College Admissions* (2010); *Rewarding Strivers: Helping Low-Income Students Succeed in College* (2010); *Improving on No Child Left Behind: Getting Education Reform Back on Track* (2008); *America's Untapped Resource: Low-Income Students in Higher Education* (2004); *Public School Choice vs. Private School Vouchers* (2003); *Divided We Fail: Coming Together Through Public School Choice: The Report of The Century Foundation Task Force on the Common School,* chaired by Lowell Weicker (2002); and *A Notion at Risk: Preserving Public Education as an Engine for Social Mobility* (2000). He is a graduate of Harvard College and Harvard Law School.

MOSHE Z. MARVIT practices both labor and employment discrimination law. He has worked at the National Labor Relations Board and was an editor at the *Employee Rights and Employment Policy Journal.*

He is the author of several recent law review articles in these areas in the *William & Mary Policy Review*, the *Transportation Law Journal*, the *Ohio Northern University Law Review*, and the *Southern University Law Review*. Additionally, he has published fiction in a number of journals, and has a book-length collection of short stories, entitled *Urbesque*, with The Green Lantern Press. He received a BA in philosophy at Penn State, an MA in political science from the University of Chicago, a JD from Chicago-Kent College of Law, and is currently pursuing a PhD in labor history at Carnegie Mellon University.

THOMAS GEOGHEGAN is a labor lawyer based in Chicago and is the author of *Were You Born on the Wrong Continent? How the European Model Can Help You Get a Life* (New Press, 2010) and *Which Side Are You On? Trying to Be for Labor When It's Flat on Its Back* (Farrar, Straus and Giroux, 1991).